The Good
Listener

compassionate

caring

healing

respectful

The Good Listener

loving

patient

attentive

James E. Sullivan

empathizing

ave maria press **Notre Dame, Indiana**

Founded in 1865, Ave Maria Press is a ministry of the Indiana Province of Holy Cross.

www.avemariapress.com

ISBN-10 0-87793-943-8   ISBN-13 978-0-87793-943-6

Cover and text design by Amy Crownover.

Printed and bound in the United States of America.

Library of Congress Cataloging-in-Publication Data

Sullivan, James E., 1920-

The good listener / James E. Sullivan.

p. cm.

ISBN 0-87793-943-8

1. Listening--Religious aspects--Catholic Church. 2. Interpersonal relations--Religious aspects--Catholic Church. I. Title.
BV4647.L56 S85 2000
248.4'6--dc21

00-008683
CIP

Contents

*This book is gratefully dedicated to my dear friends,
the late Betty Gately and Fr. Tom Mannion,
two of the world's best listeners.*

PREFACE

During my twenty-six years as director and full-time counselor at the Religious Consultation Center for the diocese of Brooklyn, I was privileged to work with hundreds and hundreds of clients: priests, religious sisters and brothers, and lay persons. They were sincere, caring people, but they were hurting—many of them hurting terribly. They were anxious, depressed, emotionally confused, and many felt trapped and helpless.

Their pain touched me very deeply. Above all, I was saddened to see the gnawing hurt that seemed to be the very core of their distress—their terribly low self-esteem. It seemed so incongruous that such wonderful people felt so poorly about themselves.

For most of them, all that I was able to do was to listen to them. I let them know that I understood how they felt, that I cared, that I didn't blame them for feeling that way. Who wouldn't feel that way in their circumstances? They weren't bad because they felt that way. They were only human!

At first, I felt that this did little good. I felt helpless before their pain. And yet, I noticed that my understanding did seem to help. Gradually, they began to feel better. They recognized that it was unfair to blame themselves for feelings that they couldn't help having.

And they began to rally their interior strengths in order to change their painful situation.

It was only slowly, however, that I grasped why my understanding had helped them. It helped to remove that part of their pain that was the most distressful: their terrible guilt and self-hatred. Being listened to had validated their painful feelings and therefore had validated and affirmed them as persons of worth.

The whole experience made me realize what an unspeakable power listening is. It is a marvelous power for good when we listen well, and, conversely, a fearful power for evil, when we listen poorly or not at all.

The reasons why listening is such a powerful force are not always very evident. The pain created when we are not heard—the sense of feeling blamed, the feelings of guilt, the tragic impulse to undo our "evil" by punishing ourselves—those feelings are mostly unconscious or semi-conscious. The same is true of the triggering mechanism which sets off the guilt, even when we have done absolutely nothing wrong. Often, we don't even realize that we feel guilty, that we are emotionally pushed to punish ourselves. We only know that we feel terrible!

Hence, the purpose of this book. For us to appreciate the healing power of listening and to rid ourselves of the unfair guilt that haunts us, we have to bring these feelings into conscious awareness. Only then can we fight the effects that the poor listening of others has had on us. Only then can we appreciate how very vital it is that we ourselves become good listeners.

I owe a huge debt of gratitude to Cathy Kelly for her insightful suggestions and for her painstaking re-working of the manuscript. I am also very grateful to Sr. Joseph Agnes, SC, for her helpful re-editing of the finished product.

CHAPTER 1

Listening: Relief From Pressure

Some years ago there was a splendid motion picture called *The Miracle Worker*. It was the story of Helen Keller, that unfortunate woman who had lost both her sight and her hearing when she was still a young child. That was a heartbreaking affliction for her, especially as she grew into adolescence and young womanhood. She had a brilliant mind, but she had no way to get others to understand what she was thinking or feeling. And others, also, were powerless to communicate with her. It was as though she were locked alone, in a cold, dark dungeon.

As a result, she grew up like a wild animal. She'd stuff food into her mouth and, when she disliked it, she'd spit it out. If anyone tried to stop her, she'd flail her arms and legs in a wild tantrum and bite their hands.

In one scene, her grandmother was feeding Helen's baby sister when Helen entered the room, holding her little rag doll. Wildly, she started to pull the buttons from her grandmother's dress. Her grandmother screamed for help, fearful that the baby would be hurt. Helen's parents and older brother came running.

Her father was overcome with grief. "Oh Lord," he cried out, "How long can we put up with this!" Her brother was cruel. "She's an animal!" he shouted. "She should be put away with the rest of the animals."

It was only Helen's mother who understood. She kept saying: "No! Wait! Wait! Helen is trying to tell us something. That's it! That's it! She wants her doll to have eyes." So she took two buttons and sewed them onto the face of Helen's rag doll. Helen reached out and felt them and the change in her was remarkable. She held her doll close and rocked it in her arms. And she sat down, calm and peaceful as could be.

What a powerful scene. It made me realize, more than ever, how desperately each one of us needs to be heard and understood, especially by the people who are dear to us. And conversely, how vital it is for us to become good listeners in order to meet that need in others.

Helen had warm, motherly feelings for her "child," her little rag doll. She wanted her doll to have the eyes that she herself could not have. And it was so frustrating for her when she couldn't get anyone to understand that. It's no wonder she went wild. Her mother's sensitivity was absolutely beautiful. In contrast to her husband and her son, she put aside her own natural assumption—that Helen was simply having a tantrum—and took on Helen's point of view instead. She entered Helen's world, and so was able to understand what Helen was feeling.

The Heart of Loving

All genuine loving begins with this attentive, sensitive listening. This is the "dying to self" about which Jesus speaks—the giving up, at least temporarily, of my own point of view. It requires turning aside for the moment, from my own perceptions, in order to be present in the world of another: to see what the other person sees, to feel what the other person feels. Few other sacrifices on my part are so difficult. And probably no other sacrifice treats you with such exquisite reverence and respect.

An Irreplaceable Kindness

The kindness of sensitive listening is the precise touch that can heal painful wounds. In her moment of rage, what Helen Keller really needed was to be heard. If her mother had given her a new doll or a chocolate bar or even a big hug, Helen would have been completely unmoved. Those gifts would have been more geared to satisfy her mother's need for peace rather than Helen's need. They would have left Helen more frustrated and she would have simply brushed them aside. What she needed was someone to understand her, to appreciate what she was feeling. That was the only thing that gave her peace. Indeed, it is the only thing that gives any one of us peace.

The truth is that our need to be heard and understood is a powerful, relentless hunger. It never diminishes. It never goes away. And how spontaneously we love and bless, with our whole heart, the one who meets this need with tenderness and care.

THE SOURCE OF LISTENING'S POWER

Why is that so? Why does it mean so very much to us that we be listened to? Because good listening fulfills three of our most deeply felt human needs, needs that cannot really be fulfilled in any other way:

1. Our need to ventilate our feelings; to find a healthy outlet for them;
2. Our need for emotional intimacy;
3. And, most important of all, our overwhelming need to have our self-esteem validated and affirmed.

Let's look at all three. We'll treat the first one here and the others in subsequent chapters.

OUR NEED FOR RELEASE

Why do our feelings need to be vented? Because our feelings—especially our strong feelings—are like scalding steam in a kettle. They are raw energy, powerful and explosive. They must find some channel of release. Otherwise their powerful energy will tear us apart, just the same as the steam would blow apart the kettle if the spout were blocked. In order to appreciate this, we need only to experience someone who is furious. He is like a wild animal, a time bomb of fearful, explosive energy. Unless that energy is "de-fused" in some healthy way, it has the potential to destroy everything in sight.

Sometimes the raw energy goes inward, causing an implosion in the form of a deep depression. Although depression sometimes has a physical cause, it is most often experienced by those who are covering up an explosive anger, an anger for which they feel so ashamed that they have to hide it even from themselves!

This powerful energy does not have to be destructive. Given the right conditions, it can be channeled into healthy, constructive activity. Consider the case of a young mother whose child's leg was caught beneath the wheel of a car. Even though she was a slight woman who weighed little more than a hundred pounds, she actually lifted the side of that mid-sized car to release her child. Her love and compassion for her little son channeled her fury in a positive and healthy direction.

This energy can also be released by sharing our burning feelings with an attentive, caring listener. This type of relief is probably the most adequate and satisfying of all. It is certainly the one that brings us the most peace.

It is not possible, however, to experience this welcome release with just anyone. I have to find a person who receives my feelings and understands them, a person who cares. It gives me almost no relief to pour out my feelings to someone who doesn't listen well, or, to someone who doesn't respect my feelings, who tells me: "Oh, you shouldn't feel that way!" That kind of a response is so frustrating that it only makes me feel worse! I can feel relieved only when my feelings are embraced and validated.

A Different Kind of Relief

Some of our strongest needs, like hunger and thirst, can find a release when they reach their objective: our hunger, for example, is satisfied with food, or our thirst with water. But most of our powerful feelings cannot be released in that way, because their objective is either unobtainable or forbidden.

So, for example, is the case with feelings of grief at the death of a dear friend. I cannot bring my friend back to life. The objective is impossible to attain. The only relief for my awful pain of loss is the comfort I receive when you understand my grief and don't look down on me for feeling it; when your care and acceptance let me know that my grief is okay—is more than okay, is a proof of my great love for my friend.

The same with my feelings of hate and jealousy or my sexual desires for another person's spouse. Those feelings cannot legitimately find their objective. I can't kill you because I hate you or feel jealous of you! The only legitimate release for those feelings is when I am able to vent them to a warm, non-judgmental listener—to a person who understands why I feel the way I do, and who doesn't blame me for feeling that way. Once I find that you listen like that, the pouring out of my feelings to you brings me great relief.

Feelings of Hate

Paul, a very sincere man, was bothered a great deal by his feelings of hate for a fellow worker, a man who had told insidious lies about him. "Father," he said to me, "I feel guilty, but I can't seem to help it. I hate his guts! I keep hoping that he'll mess up his job and get fired."

I nodded to let him know that I heard him. And, after he had expressed that pain for a while, I said to him: "Paul, how in God's name could you feel any different? This fellow really hurt you, so naturally you want to hurt him right back. You can't help that."

I waited for a few moments. He looked somewhat relieved. Then I said: "Paul, the fact is that you have not hurt him, or lied about him the way that he did about you. You're a bigger man than he is."

Paul was visibly touched. He found it a lot easier not to blame himself for his strong feelings. The awful pressure was relieved.

The Destructiveness of Unreleased Feelings

What happens to my strong feelings when I cannot find a good listener? Terrible things happen. Destructive things! My feelings in this case escape in directions that are violent and self-defeating. They either vent their energy against my body and tear it apart, or they get out sideways in ugly and self-defeating behavior.

When I can find no release for those explosive feelings, their energy smashes inward, and my body becomes torn with painful physical symptoms: high blood pressure, asthma, migraine headaches, ulcers, arthritis. These painful physical symptoms are often the result of bottled-up emotions, emotions that I can't get out in a straightforward and healthy way.

Many people seek relief from these powerful feelings by taking some alleviating medication or by burning up some of the energy in strenuous exercise. These are the "solutions" that are so common in our high-pressure culture. Our drug stores are literally teeming with pain relievers, muscle relaxants, and medications to lower blood pressure.

These steps, however, only serve to relieve the symptoms. They don't eliminate the root cause of the problem. In order to do that—to discover the instigating cause and to root it out—I must consciously identify my trapped, painful feelings and then give them the healthy, adequate expression that they need.

A TELLING EXAMPLE

In a recent film called *The Wingless Bird*, a British army captain was home on leave from the horrors of the trench warfare of World War I. He was tense beyond belief, trying his best to keep the "stiff upper lip" that his family's tradition had imposed upon him. Painfully conscious that he had to return to the front in a few days, he began to realize that he simply had to express those feelings or go out of his mind.

So he finally got up the courage to talk to his brother's wife, a beautiful young woman whom he admired and loved very much. She was the perfect one to speak to. She listened with a look of genuine understanding and care. "It's not warfare!" he blurted out. "It's absolute slaughter!"

He told her about the rain and the constant mud, the swarms of rats, the torn bodies, the sickening fear, the senseless orders from generals who kept themselves safely distant from the front lines. "I'm sorry for burdening you with this," he said. "But there is no one else I can talk to." She embraced him. "I'm so glad you told me. I'm glad that you trust me!"

His terrible tension was visibly relieved. It was so good to get it all out, to have someone understand what he was feeling, to have someone care. He was able to smile then and he quoted to her the thirty-second psalm, the psalm in which David called God "his hiding place." "That's what you are to me," he said. "You are my 'hiding place.'" Any one of us who has found such a "hiding place" for our own powerful feelings knows what a deep comfort that is.

A WORSE ROUTE STILL

When I fail to find a good listener, my trapped feelings do one of two things. They either attack my body, causing all kinds of psychosomatic symptoms, as noted before, or, worse still, they seek an avenue of escape through other channels, channels that were never meant to handle that energy. I may find myself eating too much and unable to stop, drinking too much and denying that I have a problem, or drawn almost irresistibly to psychedelic drugs or alcohol.

The root cause of all this unwelcome behavior is not some evil streak in me. It is my unresolved conflict, my locked-in feelings that cannot find a healthy outlet.

THE WORST "RELIEF"

There is one final route that my feelings can take and this is probably the most self-defeating of all: I can find myself allowing this explosive energy to break out in ugly, abrasive behavior toward others. I become sarcastic and abusive, with a constant "chip" on my shoulder. I use vulgar language and gestures. I explode into violent screaming at the slightest provocation. I become repulsive.

We need only glance at the daily newspapers to see how often this happens. People's hate and rage literally explode into cruel and vicious behavior. Impatience pushes drivers to reckless risks. Envy and jealousy turn even gentle people into treacherous schemers.

If we had the chance to study those people closely, we might well find that they are not hardened criminals. They are ordinary people who have no healthy outlet for their powerful feelings. They have no one to listen to them, no one to appreciate the agony they are going through, no one to care.

A good listener would have defused all that explosive energy, offered them unbelievable relief and peace, and allowed them to avoid the bitter regrets they now suffer.

CONCLUSION

It is very evident, then, that our need to be listened to is simply a basic and profound need—not only for our emotional health but for our physical and spiritual health as well. The good listener is a very special healer.

QUESTIONS FOR REFLECTION

1. Can you think of a specific occasion on which you felt a great sense of relief at being truly listened to? What was the issue or situation causing you distress? How did the other person communicate to you that he or she was present, listening, and understanding your feelings?

2. Can you think of a specific occasion on which you were able to listen in this crucial way to someone else? Can you think of any recent occasion on which you were able to do this?

CHAPTER 2

Listening: Friend of Intimacy

I realize now that when you listen to me—with evident understanding of my feelings, with reverence and respect for them—then the burden that you lift from me is a great relief. You defuse a great deal of the emotional pressure that could tear me apart. If your listening did nothing else for me except that, it would be a treasure!

Providing this kind of relief, however, is only the beginning of listening's healing power. As noted before, listening is also a great facilitator in helping me to achieve an even greater human need—my need for emotional intimacy and love.

FEAR OF REJECTION

As much as I hunger for love—to give love and especially to receive love—there is one huge roadblock that constantly gets in the way: my fear of rejection.

I would love to have you know me, truly, "warts and all"! I'd love to feel so completely free in your presence that I could speak out with total candor, without needing to be careful or guarded, without the fear that you might misunderstand me and look down on me, knowing that you love me just as I am.

But I'm afraid. Afraid that just the opposite will happen: that you won't understand me; that you will think that I am stupid or foolish; or worse, that you will try to get away from me as soon as you can comfortably do so.

That fear is absolutely paralyzing! It makes me close up like a clam. I don't speak about my real feelings. I search instead for innocuous topics—the weather, sports, current events—anything at all that will disguise my real feelings, whatever will hide from you what I am really like.

And, of course, you have your fears also. You don't want to look foolish either. So, most times, you are glad to join in my charade. And our conversation is as shallow as a saucer! I never really get to know you; and I make very sure that you don't get to know me.

It's so easy for us just to go along this way, like two railroad tracks, mile after mile, never crossing over, always keeping a "safe" distance between us.

AN END OF LONELINESS

It's very hard for me to break through this solid wall of fear. Once I discover, however, that you listen well, that you make a genuine effort to understand, then my awful fears begin to fade. I find that I can talk to you about myself. I offer small, carefully selected things at first, to be sure that my perception about you is correct, and then, gradually, even some of my well-guarded secrets, feelings that I'd be ashamed to admit to anyone else: my angry feelings, my jealous feelings, my sexual temptations.

The experience of your understanding and acceptance is a whole new world for me, a world of unspeakable comfort. No matter what I tell you, you don't look down on me. You don't consider me stupid or bad. You just seem to understand why I feel the way I do!

It's remarkable how free I feel now. I'm no longer watching every word. I'm not fretting that I revealed "too much" of myself. I feel relaxed in your company. I'm accepted, just as I am.

A Lonely Man

Years ago I counseled a middle-aged priest who was very depressed. His two best priest friends had died within a relatively short time of each other, and Joe missed them terribly. His other friends were good men, but they were not good listeners. They tried to "cheer him up" with jokes and stories from their seminary days, but they never gave him a chance to tell them about his feelings, especially about his great pain of loss.

Whenever he tried to express his feelings, they would cut him off: "Joe, come on! You can't live in the past. You have to let that go." They meant well, but being with them only left him lonelier.

Then, at one of our sessions, he seemed a lot more relieved. He told me that he had been talking to one of the Sisters in his parish. He said that she seemed to sense the deep hurt that he was feeling. She asked him to tell her about his two friends who had died. She wanted to know what they were like and what their friendship meant to Joe.

He said to me: "Jim, I couldn't believe how free I felt to tell her my feelings. She was beautiful. She really understood." He looked down then, as though he were ashamed to admit what he was going to tell me. "At one point I started to cry. I felt so ashamed but, you know, it didn't seem to bother her. She let me cry. It felt so good!"

That was the beginning of a beautiful friendship between them. Later on she also shared her feelings with him. Joe and she have remained close friends for these past twenty years. And he has told me often that the support of that friendship has helped him to be a better priest and a better listener.

Highway to Intimacy

Good listening is the first big step toward emotional intimacy precisely for this reason: it lessens our awful fear of rejection. Once I realize that you won't look down on me, that you won't make me feel foolish or stupid, my fear of rejection becomes less terrifying. There are no guarantees, of course, but that danger seems so much more remote!

This quality in you also makes you extremely attractive in my eyes. You are such a warm, caring person that you are a joy to be with. I find myself seeking you out every chance I get. I want to be with you as often as I can.

It's very consoling to me that, even when you disagree with me, you are still able to see my point of view. You are able to understand that I feel this way for a reason. Later on, you gently show me where my perceptions were inappropriate. But, right now, you are with me where I am, where I need you to be, at the cutting edge of my pain.

When you listen to me like this, I find myself wanting very much to do the same for you. The foundations for a genuine friendship have already been set in place. Gradually we begin to share more and more of ourselves until we become almost transparent to each other, sharing what is most precious to us: the things we love, the things we hate, our fears, our hopes, our ideals.

Love Without Understanding

There is simply nothing else that can do this: not great physical beauty or a brilliant mind or a sparkling personality. Not even expressions of love, especially when they are not rooted in clear understanding and affirmation.

A client once told me about a sister of his who would constantly tell him how much she loved him.

But, instead of making him feel good, her protestations of love only made him feel uneasy. He felt guilty because he felt so unmoved by them. He'd blame himself for being a "cold fish."

As we talked, however, it became clear that his sister had absolutely no idea of the emotional tensions he was experiencing at the time. And when he tried to share those feelings with her, she would cut him off and tell him that he "shouldn't feel that way." She meant well, but her lack of understanding was terribly frustrating for him, especially when she would then tell him how much she cared about him. He felt that she really didn't *know* him, so how could she love him?

A DIFFERENT WORLD

There is an enormous difference when I do feel heard and understood. Then I can let your love touch me and warm me. And my love for you becomes a stream of warm, beautiful feelings. I'm sure that Helen Keller never loved her mother more than at that moment when her mother understood her and responded to her need.

SOUL FRIENDS

There are very few things in this world that are as satisfying as having a real "soul friend"—someone whom I love and admire, who is on my side through thick and thin, "come hell or high water." That's the joy on earth that most closely approximates the ecstasy of heaven. Poets have never ceased to proclaim that "one who has found such a friend, has found a treasure."

And yet, friendships such as these are not simply found; they are made. And the most efficient "tool" that we have for making such friendships is our power to listen to each other with care, attentiveness, and respect.

The most common reason why so many potential friendships never get off the ground is our paralyzing fear of rejection. Rejection is so terribly painful that most of us simply won't risk experiencing it—at least until we have some pretty strong guarantees that it won't happen. The best guarantee of all is your willingness to listen to me with genuine interest and a non-judgmental attitude. Once I perceive you with those qualities, my fear of rejection is greatly lessened, and I can begin to take small risks to be open with you.

Achieving complete and genuine intimacy is, of course, a long process. Our first timid steps may happen rather quickly, but the feeling of complete ease in each other's presence, the joy and freedom that comes when two people are completely open to each other, involves a process, a process that takes time and the continued risk of honest revelation. The beginning of the process, however, is that special perception of you which gently guides me past the terrifying fear of rejection—my perception that you are a good listener; a person who really won't hurt me.

Questions for Reflection

1. Consider the two or three most important relationships in your life. How would you describe the quality of listening in those relationships—both your listening to the other person and him or her listening to you?

2. Can you think of a relationship you had in the past that suffered because of poor listening? Describe how this happened.

CHAPTER 3

Listening: Champion of Self-Esteem

MY GREATEST NEED

There is a third reason why I need so desperately to be listened to, and it is even more important than the other two. It is that urgent need to have my feelings validated and affirmed, especially my feelings of self-worth. This need—to feel good about myself—can never be stressed too strongly, because self-esteem is the very core of happiness.

When I have this feeling of self-worth, I experience a deep sense of inner peace—even when things about me go wrong. And, when I don't have it, there is just no other feeling or possession that can substitute for it! No other. Not wealth. Not power. Not even fame or pleasure. None of those things can make me feel good, if I don't feel good about myself!

Even if I have superior physical beauty, so that I'm the envy of every person that I meet, I can't really enjoy it. I simply can't believe that I am beautiful as long as my inner conviction is that I am ugly. People with anorexia are a good example. They feel fat, even when they are as thin as a pencil!

Being loved by another person is the feeling that comes closest to this consoling joy of self-esteem. But if I look closely at this experience of being loved, I notice that my greatest joy in being loved by you is how your love makes me feel about myself. When you love me, you give me a clear, unmistakable message that I am good and beautiful and noble. And that is the joy that touches me most deeply!

DEFENSES TO PROTECT SELF-ESTEEM

This is why I set up my strongest and most elaborate defenses to protect and to enhance my self-esteem. I employ my personal radar to anticipate any criticism and shoot it down before it can touch me. I use denial and projection with deadly accuracy to detect and to ward off the slightest attack on my sense of worth.

I am extremely sensitive, for example, to any hint you may make that I am not good, that I'm not bright. As soon as I am aware that you are implying that, I become terribly defensive, almost to the point of not hearing what you are really saying.

Or, if you imply that I am jealous, I deny it immediately, before you even have a chance to say why you feel that way. I may think to myself: "How dare you say that! Especially you, who are so full of envy and jealousy yourself!" I don't even admit the possibility that you may be right.

Unless I have a very healthy self-esteem, I cannot tolerate any criticism that will make me feel bad about myself. I use rationalization: "My whole purpose in taking that money was to help the poor!" Or, I use projection and attack you: "It's your problem, buddy! Don't go throwing your problems at me!" The defenses I use to protect my sense of self are huge!

WHITEWASHING HORROR

Even when we do the most inhuman and horrible acts of cruelty, we have to whitewash them and make them look as though they are really something noble. Consider the massacre that occurred at My Lai during the Vietnam war. The American soldiers there couldn't face the fact that they were slaughtering innocent civilians—women and children. Their sense of self could not possibly live with that horror. So they told themselves that they were just obeying orders—as repulsive as that was. They weren't cowardly or irresponsible, they told themselves; they were just good soldiers.

The same is true more recently with the Serbs in Bosnia. They really had no taste for all that slaughter, they insisted; they were simply being patriots who were ridding their country of deadly enemies. We human beings simply cannot live with despising ourselves!

EFFORTS TO ENHANCE SELF-ESTEEM

I will also go to almost unbelievable lengths to increase my feelings of self-worth. I'll nearly kill myself dieting just to feel a little more attractive. I'll undergo plastic surgery to make my nose thinner or my ears smaller. No sacrifice seems too great if it will make me feel better about myself!

Mary, a nurse in her early forties, was almost compulsive about getting further and further education. It wasn't just a normal desire for self-improvement or a healthy longing to be better prepared for her work. It was a restless, frantic need to prove her sense of worth. Unconsciously, she felt that the more degrees she acquired, the more certificates and accolades she accrued, the more other people would have to look up to her, and the more she could appreciate herself.

Her mother had treated her so poorly as a child—ridiculed her and put her down—that she was convinced that she was inferior, even though, in reality, she was a very bright and energetic person.

Her conviction, sad to say, was that she had to "prove" herself, that she had to show that she could master graduate studies and gain advanced degrees. It was what she accomplished that made her worthwhile, rather than the beautiful, generous person she was.

Self-esteem, next to God's grace, is one's dearest possession, one's most treasured feeling. It is the central source of joy in life; the joy that is at the heart of every other satisfaction. I either succeed at achieving self-esteem or I can forget about attaining any true happiness in this life.

THE POWER OF LISTENING

This, then, is the strongest reason of all why I need to become a good listener for others and the reason I need to find others who will listen to me. Being paid attention to, having our feelings understood and accepted: that kind of listening can do absolute marvels for our self-esteem. Being heard in that way communicates reverence and respect, respect for who we are and for what we have to give. It makes us feel very special.

When you give me your full attention, as though I were the only person in the world at that moment, I feel wrapped in warmth and care. You have taken the trouble to enter into my world and to see things from my point of view. I feel *understood*. I feel cared for. You don't judge me or blame me, the way other people seem to do. You understand me. You know what I'm feeling and you know why I feel that way. I even have the sense that you feel it all with me.

Even when I feel ashamed of my feelings, you won't let me feel ashamed! You tell me: "Jim, how could you not feel that way in these circumstances? Come on! You're not bad because you're furious. You're human, that's all."

AN AWESOME POWER

Listening, then, is an amazing power! It is an astounding two-edged sword which can cut in both directions. When I listen well, my listening can heal your pain and give you a beautiful sense of your self-worth. But, when I listen poorly, whether I want to do it or not, I put you down! I give you the impression that you are not worth hearing. I wound you in that most vulnerable area: your self-esteem. As the old Latin saying put it: *"Corruptio optimi pessima."* "When the best is corrupted, it becomes the worst!"

Listening, therefore, is truly an awesome power, a power that I cannot ignore. I cannot be neutral. The people around me will perceive me as a caring, loving person, and they will have a warm, positive feeling about themselves; or they will see me as a cold, indifferent person, and they will take my indifference personally. They will feel unattractive and dull, not worthy of my attention.

My ability to listen is a challenge. I cannot escape either the privilege or the burden.

QUESTIONS FOR REFLECTION

1. Who were the adults most important to you in your early years? How would you describe their ability to listen to you?

2. Can you think of someone you know who is a model for you of confident, healthy self-esteem? How is this quality manifested?

Chapter 4

Blame: Enemy of Self-Esteem

Although a healthy self-esteem means so much to our happiness and peace, it is really sad that most of us do not have a good self-esteem. Most of us feel rather poorly about ourselves. In varying degrees, we feel inadequate or stupid or unattractive.

There are several reasons for this. One cause is the set of twisted perceptions that have been imposed on us by our culture, perceptions which place unrealistic demands upon us. Very often, they are demands over which we have little or no control.

Our culture implies, for example, that a "real" man is one who is tall and muscular. He is handsome, according to society's standards for good looks: sharp, chiseled features, perfect teeth, and a full head of hair. And of course he should be outstanding in his business or profession at least by early middle age.

The "real" woman is the one with a trim figure and an ample bosom, beautiful hair and teeth, and flawless skin. She is confident and stylish and able to handle any combination of work, family, and personal life.

And if a person should "fail" in any of these respects—if, for example, a man is short or balding—he is tempted to feel that he is less of a man. He may be a great husband and father, honest and sincere in his business dealings, and noble in his ideals. That doesn't matter. In his feelings, those sterling qualities don't quite compensate for his lack of the cultural "standards" for manliness.

A woman may be a devoted wife and mother, sensitive and compassionate toward her friends and neighbors. If, however, she is not thin or stylish, she may feel as though she has not quite made it as a woman. She has qualities that are far more womanly than a nice figure could make her, but her false perceptions diminish her self-image.

OTHER DISTORTIONS

Not all our unrealistic demands upon ourselves come from the culture in which we are immersed. Many of our twisted demands come from poor childhood experiences: from parents or other significant adults in our childhood who, knowingly or not, imposed on us false and unrealistic demands about the person we "should" be.

Too many fathers expect their son to be the brilliant baseball player that they themselves aspired to be. And the son can sense his father's disappointment when he fails to be an outstanding player. The boy doesn't blame his father; he blames himself!

Far too many mothers want their daughter to be the "belle of the ball" and push her toward a maturity beyond her years. Very soon, the young girl takes on those same expectations for herself, just as though they were a new set of commandments. And she blames herself, unmercifully, when she "fails."

BLAME: THE CENTRAL ENEMY

The blows to our self-esteem that mostly concern us here, however, are the constant, insidious attacks upon our self-image from the blame that we experience every day. Even though we don't usually realize it consciously, our self-esteem is under a relentless bombardment of blame: blame from others; blame even from ourselves. These internal accusations simply devastate our self-esteem, because they make us feel ashamed and guilty.

BLAME FROM OTHERS

We actually experience two different kinds of blame: actual and implied. Actual blame occurs when you intend to blame me and want me to feel bad. When you ridicule me as stupid because I don't see things your way or yell at me that I am selfish because I don't fulfill your expectations—even though those expectations are unreasonable. I don't visit you every day or call you more often. I don't anticipate all the things that you want to get done. I'm not sensitive enough to your feelings or sufficiently responsive to your needs. You let me know in no uncertain terms how inconsiderate I am. You want me to feel guilty! And you fully succeed.

It isn't, however, only actual blame that crushes my feelings. Implied blame is just as efficient in making me squirm with guilt. Implied blame is found in your sarcasm that makes me wither, your disgusted looks that put me down, your harsh tone of voice, or worse, your ignoring me altogether! Even silent signs can have the same result. Your eyes that roll upward in disbelief when I express my opinion, your sigh of exasperation—all such signs silently scream: "How could you possibly be so stupid!"

Unintentional Signals

Even those signals on your part that have absolutely nothing to do with blame can communicate blame. You may have a pained look on your face because you have a headache; you may not answer my question because you didn't hear me. I perceive these signals as my fault. I feel that I must have done something to offend you. I'm not conscious of doing anything to hurt you, but that doesn't matter: I feel guilty!

The insidious part of all this is that I don't even consciously recognize that my painful feelings are feelings of guilt. That never dawns on me. I didn't do anything mean or selfish, so I don't understand how I possibly could be blaming myself as though I had done something wrong. All I know consciously is that I feel awful.

THE BLAME IS CONSTANT

During the course of an average day, most of us experience these signals of blame many, many times: at work, at home, on the subway, driving the car, shopping in the supermarket. The "blame" comes from all sorts of people. It's not only from people who dislike me and want to hurt me, but from strangers who don't even realize that they are hurting me. They are most painful, of course, when they come from loved ones.

Every time I perceive these signals of blame, I react with the same distressful feelings: feelings of discomfort, vague but painful feelings of unworthiness. I look down on myself, even when these negative feelings about myself are completely unfair because I have not done anything to deserve them. I probably undergo more discomfort and self-devaluation from these insidious attacks of blame than from any deliberate faults that I commit.

MY REFLEX TO BLAME

Why is this so? Why should I feel guilty, when I have not done or said anything wrong? Looking down on myself is terribly painful, even when there is a reason for it. But, why should I look down on myself when it's entirely unjustified? It just doesn't make sense.

That's precisely the point! These guilt feelings are not fair. They don't make sense. The whole process is the unfortunate result of a reflex that I developed during my childhood years: the reflex to blame! It is terribly important that I understand this insidious reflex, because it is the "culprit" that is responsible for at least half of my undeserved feelings of guilt.

DEFINITION

What is this reflex to blame? It is a feeling reaction of guilt that is triggered in me by any signal that I perceive as blame. Like all reflexes, my reflex to blame is not something that I control. It is an automatic response in my feelings to the stimulus of blame. A reflex, therefore, is not something that I consciously or deliberately cause to happen. It happens without any intervention of my conscious mind or will. Someone blames me—or appears to blame me—and, immediately, I experience the reaction of guilt, this vague, uneasy feeling of unworthiness.

Understanding this is a key to appreciating the tremendous need for us to listen well. So much of our diminished self-esteem is the direct effect of peoples' poor listening. We feel bad, not because we are bad. We feel bad because our reflex is reacting to the stimulus of blame that is implied when others ignore us. Let me explain.

NATURAL REFLEXES

We all have natural reflexes with which we were born. My leg, for example, will automatically kick up when my knee is hit with a blunt object. The pupil in my eye will automatically contract and grow smaller when light hits it. When the light is turned off, it will open wide and grow larger. I don't think about doing these things. I don't make a decision to do them. My leg and my eye respond automatically whenever the stimulus hits them.

When the stimulus of cold hits my body, I shiver. And when excessive heat strikes my body, I sweat. Those reactions are reflexes, natural reflexes inherent in the human body. They happen to me whether I want them to happen or not. The stimulus automatically triggers the reaction, without any awareness of my mind, without any decision of my will.

LEARNED REFLEXES

We not only have these natural reflexes. In the course of our lifetime, we also develop learned reflexes, or conditioned reflexes, which we developed either through frequently repeated experiences or, in some cases, because of a powerful, traumatic experience. So, for example, after driving for several months, I develop a conditioned reflex to the red lights of the car in front of me. As soon as I see them, my foot automatically presses the brake. If I have ever been severely burned, I have an immediate feeling of fear at the sight of fire. If a man has lied to me and hurt me deeply, I may develop an automatic suspicion of men.

Well, in my childhood, through the frequently repeated praise and blame from my parents, I developed two conditioned reflexes: a feeling reflex to praise and a feeling reflex to blame.

My parents praised me whenever they thought that I was being good. And the more good and helpful that I was, the greater was their expression of approval. As a result, any sign of praise began to mean to me that I was a good and lovable person. My whole system became conditioned to react to praise with delightful feelings of self-esteem. And therefore, a smile, a hug, a warm greeting, a person's good mood, indeed any sign of praise produced warm, pleasant feelings in me.

On the other hand, when my parents were disappointed in my conduct, they treated me in just the opposite way. They scolded me and punished me. They told me that I was bad and that I should be ashamed of myself. Their blame caused a very painful feeling in me. I not only felt deprived of their loving approval, I also felt that I deserved their scorn. I was bad. I was unlovable.

When their disapproval of me was repeated often enough in my childhood years, my whole system became conditioned to blame. And so, from that time onward, any sign of blame became a trigger that set off those same awful feelings of guilt and shame. And this happened, whether the blame was fair or not! I had developed a reflex to blame! So, blame, just by itself, became the trigger! I felt guilty simply because you looked annoyed or used a harsh tone of voice.

A Camouflaged Reaction

That's the insidious part about a reflex. It is not based on a logical chain of events. If you tell me that my friend died, for example, that realization goes first to my mind and, only secondly, does it trigger off a feeling response. I realize that my friend died, and I know that I'll be lonely without him/her. That perception touches my feelings and makes me sad. In this case, I know that I feel sad and I know why I feel sad. The whole process is conscious.

But a reflex bypasses the mind. It goes straight to the feelings. Someone blasts his horn behind me, and immediately I feel awful. My mind has no knowledge of what I did wrong. The "blame" of the horn immediately triggered the feeling of guilt.

Blame From Within

Perhaps even more tragic, this awful blame can come to me not only from others, but, as we saw earlier, it can also come from within myself. I can be my own prosecutor and judge, my own warden—and a cruel one at that.

How does this happen? I hate the pain of guilt feelings! Why would I ever prosecute myself? That's certainly an understandable question. Self-protection is a primary law of nature. Why would I heap blame upon myself, when blame causes me such awful pain?

Again, without realizing it consciously, I developed in my childhood an idealized image of the person that

I imagined I ought to be. An image that Karen Horney called "my idealized self." This "idealized self" is an unconscious picture that I have in my mind, a picture of the kind of man or woman I should be, the kind of husband or wife, the kind of doctor, lawyer, nurse, or teacher I should be. It decides for me the kind of disposition I should have, the kind of feelings I should feel, and the feelings I should not feel. And, because children tend to perceive things in "all or nothing" terms, my idealized self-image almost always became unrealistically high and demanding.

I imagine, for example, that I should not get angry when people hurt me, that I should always be serene and unperturbed. I imagine that I should never be enticed by sexual thoughts or desires. I should be the ideal husband: never frustrated by my wife or children. I should be the ideal wife: never tired, always good-humored and cheerful. I usually don't realize all this consciously, but those "orders" are there in my mind, ready to chastise me if I fail to live up to them.

And God forbid that I should ever feel envious or jealous! Even the suspicion that I might be jealous is so repugnant to me that I immediately deny it, even though the feeling of jealousy, just by itself, is not intended and, therefore, not blameworthy. My idealized self can condemn me simply for having the "bad" feeling.

Noble Ideals

It's important for us to realize that not all ideals fall into this category of neurotic demands. When an ideal is truly virtuous, that is, when it is realistic and attainable, then it is a beautiful encouragement to me to lead a mature and noble life. And so, for example, ideals like courtesy and thoughtfulness for others, truthfulness, gentleness, honesty, and kindness can lead us to greater personal excellence. Those are beautiful ideals, and parents who inculcate in their children ideals such as these are doing their children and the world an incalculable service.

Neurotic Ideals

The "ideals" that are neurotic, and, therefore, the source of senseless, unwarranted guilt, are those demands upon myself or others that are practically impossible to attain, expectations of myself that are beyond my physical or psychological powers. When expectations such as these become part of my value system, they act like a whole new set of commandments, *false* commandments, causing me unnecessary pain.

From within, their persistent voice keeps repeating: "You are ugly if you get angry. You are stupid if you make mistakes. You're not a real man if you cannot give your wife and children everything that the neighbors have. How can you call yourself a real woman when you are flat-chested!" And on and on.

I realize now that when I was a young priest my idealized self was terribly unrealistic. I don't know just where I picked up my interior demands, but I imagined that a priest should be available to his people twenty-four hours a day. He should never be tired, never feel annoyed when people make unreasonable demands upon him. He should be able to solve everyone's problems and know the answer to all questions. And, whenever I perceived myself as falling short of this "ideal," I felt awfully guilty; I was an unworthy priest.

NOT CONSCIOUS

This idealized image of ours is not fully conscious. I don't actively realize that it is there, within me, like a rigid, unfeeling judge, ready at any moment to pronounce sentence upon me. And the moment I feel any of these "forbidden" feelings, or become conscious of any mistakes I've made or physical limitations that I have, this inner judge of mine is absolutely ruthless in his/her blame and punishment.

This happens even though these feelings that I am experiencing are perfectly natural feelings, feelings that I cannot help experiencing; even though I have almost no control over my physical make-up or looks; even though every human being makes mistakes, no matter how smart he or she may be. Nevertheless, when I become conscious of these "limitations," I immediately feel guilty. I don't even recognize it as guilt. All I recognize consciously is that I feel terrible!

A Human Tragedy

The tragic truth, then, is that our self-esteem is under constant attack: attack from others and attack even from ourselves. Most of us are filled with some form of neurotic guilt, unfair and undeserved guilt. It is a human tragedy. And the full extent of that tragedy becomes more clear as we study in the next chapter the ruthless effects that guilt has upon us.

The Connection to Listening

What, then, is the connection between all this unnecessary pain and our power to listen? The answer will become more obvious in Chapter 6, where we see the crucial truth that our feelings react to poor listening as though it were blame. "I'm not worth being listened to," my inner voice concludes, "so I must be stupid or bad!" When you effectively ignore me by not listening well, I feel the same awful sense of unworthiness as if you deliberately screamed at me and put me down.

Questions for Reflection

1. Can you think of a specific situation in which you have felt blame directed toward you?

2. Can you think of a specific situation in which you (perhaps unconsciously) have subjected yourself to blame?

3. Can you think of a specific situation in which you may have communicated blame to another?

CHAPTER 5

The Effects of Blame and Guilt

What are the results of this constant blame, and the guilt that blame engenders in us? The effects are so devastating that a deep understanding of them is the greatest motivation I can have for wanting to be a good listener.

Guilt has two effects upon us, effects that are both painful and destructive. First and foremost, guilt wreaks havoc with my self-esteem. I come to look down on myself and despise myself. It is an excruciating feeling that can leave me so depressed that I just don't know what to do with myself. Eventually, I may not feel like eating or drinking; I may not want to talk to my family or friends; I may just want to shut down.

Second, guilt makes me feel a powerful urge to punish myself, to make myself suffer. This is difficult for most of us to comprehend. If I feel so bad already, why should I want to make myself suffer even more?

A Terrible Paradox

It's a ghastly feeling for me to feel that I am no good. It's hard enough for me when others look down on me. At least in those cases, though, I can say to myself: "Those people just don't understand you. They don't realize that you acted for good motives." And that thought brings me some peace. I'm not as bad as others think I am!

But, when I despise myself, then there is no healthy avenue of escape. That's why I feel so terribly depressed when I feel guilty. I'm stuck with being ugly and unlovable. I just want the whole world to go away; I want to blot out the pain!

As strange and incongruous as it may sound, the only means at my disposal that can lessen this awful depression is to punish myself! To "undo," to try to "pay back" for the "evil" that I have done.

So this is *exactly* what I try to do. Without even intending to, I actually set up punishments for myself. This process is almost totally unconscious, but I do actually arrange to make myself suffer. It's not that I want more pain! I don't. The reason I punish myself is to use this new pain as a bribe to take away that other pain, the scalding pain of guilt, the awful loathing of despising myself. I'm really seeking a release from pain by choosing a lesser pain to replace the greater pain.

A "Bargain" With My Guilt

I say, in effect, to the pointing finger of guilt: "Okay! You're right; I'm no good! I admit it. I do deserve to be punished. But, look! I am being punished. I'm punishing myself! So, stop pointing that ugly finger at me! I'm not all bad. At least I'm honest. I'm no hypocrite. Let me feel good at least about that!"

This kind of "reparation" would make sense if I were really guilty of an offense against God or my neighbor. A healthy and mature sense of responsibility demands that I repay you for the injury that I have caused you. It would be manifestly unjust on my part if I did not make such amends! In the case of the guilt that we are considering here, however—neurotic guilt—the unfair guilt that I assume simply because you blamed me, such self-punishments are as unjust and self-defeating as the neurotic guilt that caused them.

DOUBLE-PRONGED PUNISHMENTS

How do I punish myself? I do it in two ways. First, I push love away from me—hard to believe and very sad, but true! I reject all compliments. I just can't allow myself to accept them. Of course, I want them! But when I feel guilty, I simply cannot let myself enjoy them. I squirm when you compliment me. I'm terribly uncomfortable when you offer me affection. Yes, I do want and need affection. But when I feel guilty, I simply cannot allow myself to have it. Because, if I did, I would only feel more guilty. I'd not only feel the original guilt feelings, but now I'd feel like a hypocrite as well. I'm allowing your affection to tell me that I am good, when the "truth" is that I am bad.

So, I won't let you do nice things for me. I blunt every act of kindness that you offer. I may be glad to do kind things for you, but I won't let you reciprocate. I sense that this frustrates you, but I can't help myself. I can't let you treat me as though I were someone good, when I believe just the opposite to be true.

TYPICAL EXAMPLE

John was one of the finest men that I had ever met. He was extremely kind and thoughtful of others. He'd listen for hours to the painful experiences that they would relate. But he refused to allow others to be nice to him. He was noticeably uncomfortable with compliments, and would change the subject, almost immediately, when someone implied that he was a great person.

It was sad! John was sexually abused as a young boy and, like so many who are abused, he blamed himself rather than the man who abused him. And those neurotic guilt feelings made him so uncomfortable that he simply could not allow any affection to touch him. There were literally hundreds of people who loved and admired him deeply, but he could not let their warmth touch him.

Any counselor can recite case after case of clients who punish themselves in this way. Wives allow themselves to be treated shamefully—not only by their husbands but often even by their own children. Employees cringe when their work is noticed and praised. Good, gentle people simply won't allow themselves any joy and freeze at any sign of affection. They are convinced that they don't deserve any love or attention. And when it is forced on them, they only feel more guilty.

SET UP PUNISHMENTS

The second way that I punish myself is by actually setting up painful experiences for myself. My goal, as we saw, is to use these self-inflicted punishments as a "bribe" to replace the burning pain of despising myself.

I do this in various ways: I push myself into the background. I put myself down. I ridicule myself. I make stupid, obvious mistakes—mistakes that make people laugh at me. I even laugh with them. I say: "That was dumb, wasn't it!" I may refuse to take care of myself, eating poorly or reflecting in a sloppy appearance the antipathy I feel for myself. "That's good enough for me," I say to myself. I treat myself terribly.

It happens so often. Bright young men and women present themselves as clumsy and stupid and bungling. Students quit college just months before they are to get their degree. Men and women allow themselves to be used in romantic relationships. They send out signals to everyone around them that it is perfectly all right to take advantage of them.

Their friends may try to get them to treat themselves better. It's no use. Unconsciously, they prize their sufferings because their sufferings bring them some relief from their greater, hidden pain of self-hatred.

So the guilt that blame triggers in me is terribly painful. Painful in itself, because it lowers my self-esteem; and painful in its consequences, because it pressures me to refuse love, pressures me to punish myself.

REAL GUILT VERSUS NEUROTIC GUILT

It is very important for me to understand, as mentioned before, that not all guilt is an emotional distortion or unjust, nor are all self-restraints or self-punishments. There is a vast difference between neurotic guilt and real guilt. Real guilt—the pain that I feel when I deliberately commit sin—is not destructive. On the contrary, it is very healthy.

Why is this so? How can we say that something so painful can be healthy? Because real guilt is the direct result of my being a conscientious and responsible adult. When I deliberately hurt you, I should be ashamed of myself. I should want to undo my wrong! It is only just and fair that I apologize to you and make amends in every way that I can.

So real guilt is healthy for a number of reasons. First, because it is the direct consequence of a mature and healthy sense of responsibility. Second, because the pain that it causes instills in me a healthy dread of sin. It therefore helps to keep me from ugly, anti-social behavior. And, finally, real guilt is healthy, because in real guilt, I realize what I am feeling. I know clearly that I feel guilty, and I know why I feel that way. I know that I have done something wrong, something that needs to be undone. I know that I should be punished.

Recognizing this, i.e., that I truly am guilty, makes it easier for me to deal with my feelings in a conscious and realistic way. I can apologize to you for the disparaging things that I said to you. I can pay back the money I have stolen from you. I can thus undo for the evil that I have done. And then—and this is terribly important—I can forgive myself! I can let the guilt go and be at peace again.

NEUROTIC GUILT

Neurotic guilt, however, is very different. This is the guilt I feel simply because you blamed me, even though your blame is unfair. I have not done anything wrong. Or I feel guilty because I am misreading your innocent signals as though they imply blame. Or, the blame is coming *from inside* myself—from my unrealistic idealized self. This kind of guilt is very unhealthy and very destructive.

When I am dealing with neurotic guilt, I am not the sinner; I am the victim, the victim of a terrible injustice. Although I have done nothing evil to deserve this pain, nevertheless I suffer all the ugly consequences of guilt. And because I have not done anything wrong, I don't even realize that the discomfort I am feeling is guilt. I don't realize that I am punishing myself! And therefore I never get the satisfaction that I have paid back for my "evil." On the contrary, the whole process of self-punishment keeps going on and on and on!

Relief So Difficult

Susan, an attractive young woman in her early thirties, and a highly successful high school teacher, managed to get herself into one abusive situation after another. She came for counseling after her husband had beaten her severely. And yet, from the moment I had completed the intake interview, I was convinced that she would not remain in counseling long enough to gain insight into her behavior. Nor would she do anything in order to change her pattern of entering into such self-defeating relationships. Getting herself punished had become a sad, neurotic way of finding relief from guilt that she never should have felt in the first place.

Susan hated her father, who had often beaten her as a child. It was a hatred that would have been understandable to anyone else, but not to Susan. She felt such guilt for hating him that she "had" to punish herself by seeking out men who were just like her father. It was her way of denying her feelings of hatred and, at the same time, a way of arranging to get herself punished for them.

Her husband at the time was her third husband in the relatively short span of nine years. All three of them had been cruel to her and physically beat her. Her friends had implored her not to date them; certainly not to marry them. But to no avail! Susan admitted to her friends: "I'm not attracted to men who are kind. The only men who excite me are the men who stand up to me!"

My acceptance of her and my efforts to be kind only made her feel uneasy. She quit counseling after five sessions and went back to her abusive husband. This is one of the most tragic results of neurotic guilt: the fact that it is so difficult for its victims to gain insight and to change. So, the punishment continues, on and on! They seem never to get any relief.

The Goal of This Book

The main purpose of this book is to increase our awareness of this tragic and unjustified suffering in our lives. If we understand its roots in the constant and various kinds of blame that we experience, we will come to appreciate the place of listening in this whole process—both as a tool for healing, when we listen well, and as just another source of blame, when we listen poorly or not at all!

Have you seen this dynamic of self-punishment at work in your own life? Have you seen it in the life of someone close to you?

CHAPTER 6

Poor Listening: Insidious Blame

An understanding of the conditioned reflexes that we have developed in our childhood is probably the best clue we have for appreciating the unspeakable power of listening, both its power to build up our self-esteem and its power to tear it down.

We are all "wired," so to speak, in such a way that a vital bridge can be wired with dynamite by enemy soldiers. There is no damaging explosion when you push my praise button. On the contrary, I feel great! Your smile, your look of joy when you see me, your compliments, your warm handshake, your hug—all these are signs of praise to my feelings, signs that I'm good and bright, that I'm a lovable person.

But once you push my blame button, wow! A "dynamite" charge of guilt explodes beneath my self-esteem and shatters it. It happens so quickly. You criticize me because you don't like what I've said. You're annoyed that I laugh too loudly, that I talk too softly. That I drive too closely to the car in front of me. You're upset that I forgot the milk at the store. Anything that even hints of blame! And immediately I feel the painful twinge of guilt apart from the merit or fault in anything that I might have done or failed to do!

THE PLACE OF LISTENING

What does all this have to do with listening? It has everything to do with it. Everything! Why? Because good, sensitive listening comes across to my feelings as praise. Very special praise! And therefore it makes me feel affirmed and worthwhile. Not only are my ideas okay, I'm okay!

When you give all your attention, as though I were the only person in the world at that moment—and that's what good listening communicates to me—you touch me very deeply. You have taken the trouble to enter into my world and to see things from my point of view. I cherish that. I feel understood. I feel cared for. You don't judge me or blame me. There isn't one of us who doesn't want to be understood and accepted in this way.

It's interesting to note that your careful listening touches me more deeply that any word of praise that you could possibly say. Words are easy to say. They do not require the effort and the complete self-giving that listening requires. Words, therefore, are suspect as possible flattery.

You may have the most sincere intentions in the world. You know that I'm feeling bad and you'd like very much for me to feel better. So you tell me how good I am, how noble. But it hardly touches me. I admire you for what you are trying to do, but I don't feel any better about myself. On the other hand, when you listen to me, when you understand my feelings and thus validate them, then I am deeply moved. Your praise in listening is much more indirect, but, perhaps for that very reason, it is less suspect.

POOR LISTENING IS BLAME

Poor listening, on the other hand, does just the opposite. You are not paying attention to me. You look impatient, annoyed. You do your best to change the subject. Those signals on your part push my "blame" button. In effect, you are telling me by your aloof attitude that I am not worth listening to, that I don't have any ideas or feelings that are of any value.

The results are the same as though you blamed me directly! Immediately, I experience vague feelings of unworthiness. I may even feel selfish for wanting to talk about myself, when evidently there is nothing interesting about me to relate. I feel awful. Unfortunately, my reflex to blame is even more sensitive than my reflex to praise.

You may have no intention of sending me such a damaging message. You may be just tired or distracted by your own worries. So there may be no intended blame. That doesn't help me. My feelings see your lack of concern as my fault. There's something wrong with me!

The insidious part of all this is that my feeling is uncomfortable but it is vague. I'm not aware that my feeling is created by unfair and inappropriate guilt. And, because blame is so widespread, most of us suffer a great deal of this unfair guilt. Unfortunately, we also cause a lot of this pain in others—even though we don't intend to do so!

We must try very hard therefore to bring this insight to our conscious awareness. Let's not forget that a reflex is automatic. You push the doorbell, and the bell rings. Similarly, you blame me, and I feel guilty. And, unconsciously, I start to punish myself. I have a vague, uneasy feeling that I must pay back. It's automatic!

Choice, truth, fairness: they simply don't enter into the picture. Your accusation about me doesn't have to be true. It doesn't have to be fair. I could have just done something that was noble, but if you yell at me for doing it, I immediately and automatically feel that I am bad.

Some years ago I offered to carry a heavy package for a young woman. To my chagrin, my offer completely backfired. Instead of being pleased by my offer, she screamed at me: "You chauvinist pig!" I felt absolutely awful, as though I had deliberately insulted her. Her blame had turned my act of courtesy into an insulting gesture. And, for the moment at least, I felt just as bad as if I had intended to insult her.

It is important for us to note that it is not only severely neurotic people who have developed this reflex to blame. It is all of us! Even the most healthy among us suffer from some neurotic guilt when we are subjected to blame in all its various forms.

As Sigmund Freud put it very succinctly: "Neuroses [at least in some mild form] is the price that we have to pay for civilization." Even the best parents have to put restrictions on their children, have to impose standards of behavior. They would be very remiss as parents if they failed to do this. Their children would grow up without a healthy sense of responsibility.

The only efficient tools that parents have for building this kind of noble character in their children are the tools of praise and blame. Praise is the best reward for good behavior; blame the most effective punishment. But since all small children see things as "all or nothing," they feel bad and inadequate when they are corrected. And when corrections are repeated, as they have to be, even healthy children develop a feeling reflex to blame.

With the help of some form of counseling—a book such as this one, for example, or loving attention from a good listener—most adults are able to see their neurotic guilt feelings for what they are. Hence, after the first twinges of guilt, they are able to catch themselves and realize that they did not do anything wrong. They can say to themselves: "Hey, I'm not bad because my boss has a bad day and is yelling at me. It's his problem—not mine!" Now that's a healthy resolution to our unfair guilt feelings.

CONCLUSION

I realize now what devastating effects blame can have on me—how it sets off in me those vague, uncomfortable feelings that I am bad and that, somehow or other, I have to pay back for the "evil things" that I have done. I also see more clearly how I try to "pay back." I push love away from me, love that I'm craving but feel I don't deserve. And I set up other ways to make myself suffer. I do things and say things that make me look foolish. I allow people to take advantage of me and use me. And, tragically, this can happen even when I have not done anything wrong. Blame, just by itself, sets the whole process in motion.

What I have not realized up to now is that one of the most insidious forms of blame is poor listening. When you don't listen to me, you send me a clear message that I am not worth listening to, that I am inadequate and of little or no value. And the whole ugly process of self-punishment begins. And sadly, I can do the same thing to you.

QUESTIONS FOR REFLECTION

1. Can you think of a situation in which you have interpreted poor listening as blame?

2. Can you describe a situation in which you now realize that you communicated blame to someone else by listening poorly?

CHAPTER 7

The Ways That We Listen Poorly

It is frightening to me when I realize the serious damage I can cause you by not listening to you. The appalling message that I send—whether I mean to or not—is that you are not worth my time or my interest.

I must try to raise my awareness about this. It will be helpful if I first examine in detail the various ways in which I can fail to listen adequately. It's easy for me to slip into these bad habits without any awareness of the pain I am causing you. Unfortunately, there are at least five ways that I can do this:

1. Refusing to listen
2. Pretending to listen
3. Listening without patience
4. Listening but not understanding
5. Listening without an adequate response

Let's take time to look at each below.

REFUSING TO LISTEN

The first and most obvious way is that I can refuse to listen to you at all. "I don't want to hear it!" I tell you.

"I'm sick of your complaints!" Or, more subtly, "Not now; I don't have time." I simply refuse to give you a chance to explain how you feel or why you feel that way.

When I stop to think, it is easy for me to see how very frustrating this is for you. I may not mean to blame you, but that's exactly what my lack of interest does to you. I put you down. I communicate that you are not worthy of my time.

This kind of stonewalling happens all too often between married couples. "I need to explain," a husband will say. "You've turned me off and it's all a misunderstanding." But she won't let him talk. "No!" she says. "I'm sick of hearing your excuses!"

This is terribly frustrating for spouses in their relationship with each other. The rejected person feels alienated from the person he or she loves. Sadly, this is entirely unnecessary. If misunderstood spouses could only explain! But they are locked out.

Our friends can do the same to us, and we can do it to them. "I need you to understand," my friend says, only to hear: "I just don't have the time right now." I'm shutting you out. And that strikes your feelings exactly like blame. It's the same as my saying: "You have absolutely nothing worthwhile for me to hear!"

CHECKING MYSELF

I don't like to believe that I could do this to people, but, if I am honest, I may realize that I do. I may be more subtle about it, allowing others to talk on but not paying any attention. But that's only adding hypocrisy to my stonewalling! I must ask myself honestly: "Is there anyone in my life that I treat this way? Spouse? Friend? Fellow worker? Neighbor?"

It's true, of course, that fruitless discussions can be very frustrating. But let me ask myself: "Why were they fruitless? Was either of us too defensive? Am I sure that I really heard your frustration? Did I feel that you were lying to me?" Then, let me try to correct what's wrong. I can say to you: "Okay, I'll be glad to talk it over with you, but if you tell me something that I know is not true or is just intended to hurt me, then I won't be able to continue."

PRETENDING TO LISTEN

The second way that I can be a poor listener is more devious. I can pretend to listen to you, when I'm not really listening at all. This also happens a lot.

Often, leaders of big corporations will give questionnaires to their employees, asking for their opinions and suggestions. They give the appearance of being interested. But so often it is only a charade! They have no intention of considering the suggestions. They don't even read them.

Parents sometimes do this to their children. They pretend to listen, but they don't allow for any possibility that their son or daughter might be right. Their mind is made up. So they block out, beforehand, all the ideas and the feelings that their children will present. Their "listening" is a sham.

And, of course, children are often guilty of this same offense with their parents! Some teenagers have developed pretense into an art form. "Let the old man talk. I'll just humor him and then I'll do as I please." It's an insult to the father. And it triggers off in the father the same painful consequences as blame. It makes the father feel like a fool.

Something like this happened to me years ago, when I was a seminarian. I was talking to another student who was pretending to listen. He would nod and say, "Hmm-hmm," but he didn't even look at me. He kept looking around at what the other seminarians were doing. So, just to test it out, I said to him rather facetiously: "Yes, so I decided to stab the Rector." He just kept on nodding and saying, "Hmm-hmm, yes. How interesting!" He hadn't heard a word that I was saying. I stopped, feeling foolish.

I hate to think that I have ever acted this way in my conversations. I'd certainly feel ashamed of myself. But, that's the precise reason why I tend to block out such behavior from my consciousness! Let me be brutally honest with myself. When was my listening a pretense? When was my mind miles away when you were talking to me?

The third way that I can fail at listening is to listen but without exercising the necessary patience that real listening requires. I refuse to give you the time that you need to get all of your thoughts and feelings sorted out. In this instance, I listen, but I resent the fact that you are taking up my time. So I keep interrupting you with quick "solutions" for your problem. What I really want is a "quick fix" so I won't have to listen to you any further. You tell me about a difficult and complicated problem at work, and I respond with: "Just tell the supervisor that you want a transfer to another department. Show him that you're not going to put up with that nonsense any more!" And I say this without having any idea what the real problem is.

It could be that you are too timid, that you need the encouragement to speak up for yourself. I might be right in concluding that you send out signals that invite others to take advantage of you. True! But, there may be many other reasons for your trouble. It might be that you are completely misunderstanding your fellow workers. It could be that you have a "chip" on your shoulder and give off an attitude that simply invites hostility from others. It might even be that you hate your job and would be much happier in another setting. I simply don't know the real reason until I give you the time and the patience to talk it all out! I first have to feel your pain and let you know that I understand and care. But, I'll never be able help you to change until I listen closely enough to understand your real problem.

Quick Reassurances

Sometimes I express my impatience by too-quick reassurances. I say, "Don't worry. Your son is going to be all right!" without having any idea whether or not that is true. Or I'll simply agree immediately and totally with anything you say: "Oh yes, yes. Oh, you are so right. Yes. Yes." That's exactly the same as if I said: "Will you keep quiet!" Exactly the same! I don't want to listen, and I am just trying to hurry you off.

Honest Limitations

Granted, there are occasions when we honestly do not have the time to listen. But, in those cases, we should say that. You might say, "Gee, I'm sorry, but I have an appointment fifteen minutes from now. But I want to hear what you have to say. Could we get together tomorrow morning, say about ten o'clock?"

That's both honest and kind. It is being respectful to ourselves and to the person with whom we have the appointment. And, it is also being kind to the person wanting to be heard. Much more kind than if I stayed for a few minutes and was so anxious about my appointment that my nervousness showed all over. When I explain why I can't listen now, you don't feel rejected or ignored.

There may also be times when your ventilation of your feelings is not purposeful or directed. Times when you just talk endlessly, compulsively—splattering feelings all over the place, jumping from one painful situation to another. In this instance, it is not only very painful for me to listen to you, but your undirected ventilation doesn't do you any good either. So, once I sense that this is the case, then the kindest thing for me to do is to stop you momentarily and help you to focus.

I can say: "I'm awfully sorry for what you're going through, but I'm not sure what's really hurting you the most. Are you feeling that your husband doesn't really care about you anymore? Is that what really hurts?" I help you to bring the real issue into focus. Only then can my understanding and care really touch you.

In both of these instances, I am really listening very well. I'm simply guiding the conversation into focus, so that your painful feelings move toward a goal and both you and I can get a better understanding of how you're hurting.

LISTENING BUT NOT UNDERSTANDING

The fourth way that I can fail as a listener is to listen to you but fail to understand what you are really feeling. This is an especially painful experience for you. And yet, it's almost unbelievable how often this happens, even among people who sincerely want to be good listeners.

George, for example, was a married man in his early fifties. He felt very depressed because his new boss at the office not only failed to appreciate his long experience with the company, but, even worse, because he treated George like an office boy. It really hurt him, especially at that stage in his life when he couldn't easily get another position.

George kept all this to himself for a while, feeling a little ashamed of his hurt. "Men should be above such things!" Eventually, however, he couldn't stand it any longer, so he tried to tell his wife. It was a disaster! She cut him off by telling him what happened on the soap opera that afternoon.

He was furious. "Damn it, Mary, will you listen!" Then she felt hurt. Her reply was blistering. "I'm sick of your self-pity. Do you think that you're the only one who has things hard?" He was devastated! The blow to his self-esteem was so great that he couldn't talk. He just closed down.

Husbands, of course, can be just as cruel. Jane was a woman in her forties, who felt that the woman next door to her was a good friend. One day, however, that woman gave a party for all the neighbors on the block but didn't include Jane. She was terribly hurt and was immediately haunted with self-doubt: Why wasn't she invited? What was wrong with her?

She tried to talk about it with her husband that evening. To his credit, he tried to support her, but he misunderstood badly. He said: "Jane, you don't need her for a friend! You have plenty of friends. Honest to

God, you let the darndest things upset you!" It was awful. In one sweeping statement he trivialized all her pain, as though she were a silly little girl who let insignificant things bother her. What a blow to her self-esteem!

In both of these cases, the person's sense of self was literally shattered! Both were being blamed for the way they felt instead of being heard and understood and embraced. Both of them were put down brutally, and it was by someone they loved!

OUR MOST COMMON FAILURE

This is the type of failure at listening that well-meaning people can make most often. And, whether we like to admit it or not, you and I have fallen into this category. We thought that we were listening, but we weren't listening to our loved ones. We were listening to ourselves, to our own point of view.

We'll see more of this later, but, at least, let us note it now. The biggest reason for our failure to listen well is our failure to enter into the other person's world, our failure to see their problems from their point of view. We don't look at their problem through their eyes. We look at it through our own!

I cannot see what you see or feel what you feel if I stand here facing you. I've got to go to where you are, and face the way you are facing. I've got to look at your world through your eyes. If some obstacle is a mountain to you, I'm being brutal if I say: "Ah! It's really only a little molehill." Unless I see a mountain, I haven't really heard you!

Later on, I can try to help you to see that your fears are unrealistic, that what you see really is a molehill. But, not until I have first seen it as a mountain! And felt your fear. And understood your anxiety. Only then can I walk with you to the molehill. Before that moment, you feel nothing but blame, just because you see a mountain and no one else does!

Listening Without an Adequate Response

The final way that I can fail at listening is to hear you but fail to give you an adequate response. When I do that—when I don't let you know that I understand what you are feeling—it's just as though I didn't hear you at all! There's no comfort for you. You're left with your confusion and your pain.

You don't know how I feel about what you've told me. You have no idea whether I understand or not, whether or not I'm looking down on you or judging you. You took the risk of trusting me with your feelings, and now I've left you alone in "no man's land," with unbearable anxiety.

When I do this, even though I have listened to you, my listening is worthless! It's like penicillin that I keep locked up in my closet while you are dying of pneumonia. My care and understanding doesn't do you a bit of good. And yet, there are people who "listen" this way. They remain completely non-committal. It's cruel. I not only fail to give you the support that you need but my bland coldness becomes an attack upon you, a putdown. Your feelings hear my silence as blame. You don't conclude that there is something lacking in me. You're convinced that there is something wrong with you!

A Shining Example

There was a Sister in one of our groups at the office years ago who beautifully exemplified what a warm, understanding response could mean to people who are hurting. I noticed that whenever any member of the group had something painful to relate, that person would always look at her.

A person just had to see her to understand why. She showed such great empathy on her face. She nodded with understanding. And with a tone of great warmth, she would tell the hurting persons how bad she felt for them. She let them know that she was in their world, that she understood and cared. Her outward expression of her empathy left them without any doubt that she was with them in their pain.

Conclusion

In summary then, poor listening does more harm than most people ever dream. It sends a strong message to you that there is something wrong with you. I must be brutally honest with myself here. Most poor listeners have no idea that they are poor listeners.

Their own defenses convince them that they are really good listeners. But in reality, they are constantly responding to their own point of view and they think that they are responding to us.

My own defenses are very active also! I want to think of myself as a good listener and a kind person, so that's what I pretend to myself that I am. It takes a lot of honest searching for me to find the truth. I need to determine to look closely at all the ways by which I can fail as a listener and very honestly check up on myself.

It will help me no end to ask my close friends to be brutally honest with me in this regard. Do I listen well to them? Have they felt understood and cared for by me? Do I pick up their real feelings? Do I give them time or am I usually in a hurry?

If I truly want to be a good listener, I have to pay this price!

QUESTION FOR REFLECTION

Consider again the five ways in which we can fail to listen well:

1. Refusing to listen
2. Pretending to listen
3. Listening without patience
4. Listening but not understanding
5. Listening without an adequate response

Which of these do you struggle with most often? Give a specific example of how this manifests itself.

CHAPTER 8

The Steps to Good Listening

We have touched on a number of kinds of poor listening. What we need to focus on now are the ways that we can fight those inconsiderate lapses and learn instead to listen and listen well. There are four crucial steps to good listening:

1. Stepping out of my own world
2. Entering into your world
3. Sensing your deepest feelings
4. Giving an adequate response

1. STEPPING OUT OF MY OWN WORLD

The first and foremost requirement is that I must step out of my own world, my own thoughts and feelings. I have to put aside—at least for the moment—my own preconceived notions and prejudices and my own point of view. This is an essential step, and it is no easy task!

Why is this so hard? Because my own needs and feelings beat like a heavy pulse inside me. They absolutely demand my attention. My own pain, my own need to be understood, my own need to be affirmed, scream for my attention. My point of view is also demanding. It makes me feel that there simply cannot be any other way of looking at things than the way in which I see them. So, I am tempted to give absolute attention to my own perceptions and feelings, to remain completely caught up in my own evaluations of what has been said or done.

And yet, for me to hear and understand you, I have to break out of this world of mine, or I will never see things as you see or feel what you feel! I'll never be able to meet your need for understanding and care.

Now, I don't have to leave my own world forever. There are times, after all, when I need to be listened to. If I always put aside my own point of view, I violate my own integrity as a person. And, in fact, I don't have to do that in order to be a good listener. What I must do is to leave my own world for the space of time that I am listening to you.

We must also recognize that stepping out of my own does not mean that I have to agree with you. I have a right to my own ideas, and my own ideas may be correct! Being a good listener simply means getting to see what you are seeing, so that I can understand what you are experiencing and feel it with you. You need me to be true to you; you don't need me to be untrue to myself. Happily, there is no real conflict here. I am able to do both. I am able to understand what you are feeling, even though I am convinced that your feeling is exaggerated and inappropriate. When I understand that and feel that pain with you, I am not saying that you are right. I am saying that I understand why you feel the way you do.

Granted, it is very hard for me to do this, especially when my perception of the truth is different from yours. It takes a lot of concentration on my part to make sure that I'm really hearing you, as well as a lot of sensitivity and generosity. It is truly a "dying" to myself. But, there is no other way to begin the process of careful listening.

2. ENTERING INTO YOUR WORLD

This brings us to the second essential requirement for good listening. I must not only leave my own world, but I must also enter into your world, understand your point of view, and see your world as though I were looking at it through your eyes.

If I think that a coming exam is easy to take, I can't imagine that you think it is hard. So, I can't understand your anxiety or feel for you! To do that, I have to look at the exam through your eyes. For you, the danger of failing is real. I may know how smart you are, so I'm convinced that you will pass with flying colors. But that is not what is important right now. I need to focus on your feelings.

Or, your wife's promotion may be a joy for her, but for you it's a real sadness because it will take her away from the home more often. If I am going to understand your feelings, I have to see that absence for what it means to you. I may feel overjoyed for your wife. That promotion is a great boost to her self-esteem, a boost that I know she really needs. But I must put all that joy aside for the time that I am listening to you.

Again, we must remember that this is not easy. Entering your world is a very difficult thing for me to do at any time because I am so convinced that my own perception is the true one. And it is even when my feelings about myself get involved, when, for example, you misunderstand my good intentions and blame me. When you see my offer to help you with your income tax as my implying that you are stupid and not able to do it by yourself, I feel hurt by your rash judgment. My first impulse is to defend myself. But, when I do that, I'm not hearing you; I am not respecting your pain. I need to enter your world and see that, for you, my offer to help you was an insult.

My efforts to enter your world become even more complicated when you intentionally hide your true feelings. Our "idealized selves" often look upon negative feelings as repulsive and bad. So, immediately, often unconciously, we hide them from ourselves—and from others.

At one session of group counseling years ago, a man in his forties expressed to the group how empty his life was. He was a social worker and was constantly helping other people. But no one ever seemed to sense his needs or reach out to him. A woman in the group felt his pain very deeply and in the most warm and gentle manner, she leaned forward and said to him: "Joe, you're lonely!" It was beautiful, compassionate feedback. But not for Joe. He all but shouted, in a voice dripping with annoyance: "I am not!" Loneliness, in his eyes, was something shameful, so he had to deny it.

It's hard enough for me to enter your world, even when you want me to be there with you, but it becomes much more difficult when, in shame and fear, you make great efforts to hide your true feelings from me. So, in my efforts to understand you, I cannot rely only on what you say in words. I have to observe how you look, your mannerisms, your tone of voice. I need to use more than my ears. I need to rely on my eyes and my heart as well. I need to search your face for possible lines of tension, even while you lips are telling me that all is well. I need to notice your body language—your stiffness, your sitting sideways that speaks of your withdrawal, your folded arms that wall you off from me, your avoidance of eye contact, your forced smiles that mask your anger and your shame.

I need to listen also with my heart. How would I feel if my dear friend died? Deeply sad. Then, why is this person acting so nonchalant after losing her mother? What would I be like if someone told vicious lies about me? I'd be furious with him and want to tell him off! Then, why is my fellow worker acting as though it doesn't bother him that a friend betrayed him and ruined his reputation?

When I listen to you with my heart, I can more readily detect your denial and better understand the depths of your shame and your guilt. Then slowly, gently, I can help you to get past it. When you are ready, I can say: "Wow, I'd be furious at that guy!" I can model for you to let you feel that your anger is okay!

3. Sensing Your Deepest Feelings

The third requirement for being a sensitive listener is not as important as the first two, but it is still very helpful for relieving your pain. It is my effort to search for your deepest hurt: the thing that bothers you the most.

When you are hurting, there are, usually, a number of things that are bothering you. Your husband leaves his dirty clothes on the floor. He doesn't cover his mouth when he coughs. He doesn't hold your chair for you. And when you talk to him while he's watching the ball game on TV, he only half listens to you.

All of those things are hurtful to you. And when I respond to any one of them with understanding and care, that response is a big help to you. But, I help you the most when I am able to identify your deepest pain and respond to that with understanding and support. How do I do this? By realizing that, almost always, the worst hurt is the hurt to your self-esteem. Underlying all your other pains is the feeling that you have been stupid or bad, or the dreadful feeling that you are powerless to change your painful situation.

It's very consoling for you when I appreciate that special hurt and respond to it. I don't overlook your other pains. I certainly understand how hard it is to live with an inconsiderate husband. But then I can add, "I wonder if all this makes you feel that you don't really matter to him!" I help you to name this pain which certainly must be the deepest of all. And I try to respond to that blow to your self-esteem, and to the guilt that you feel for being so angry at him.

Perhaps your friends are making bigger and bigger salaries, while you seem to be going nowhere in your career. Your friend interrupts you with some inconsequential remarks when you are trying to share with him an experience that is very meaningful to you. All of these things are hurtful in themselves. But the bottom line is what these hurts are saying to you—that you are not worth too much, that you are really inferior. So it means a lot to you when I let you know that I appreciate that. Then my listening and my response become truly sensitive.

Some years ago I was counseling Tom, a middle-aged high school teacher, who felt very bad that he was not appointed to be the new principal. Most of the faculty members had expected that he would be the one chosen—including Tom himself. Many painful feelings tore at him: hurt, that somehow he had let down his family and friends; anger, because the appointment was evidently motivated by "politics" rather than by merit; embarrassment, when the other faculty members asked him, "What happened?" as though he had some secret limitation that impeded his chances.

All of those feelings were painful. I sensed, however, that his greatest pain was his feeling that he was incapable and inadequate. I felt that hurt with him very deeply, and I knew that, at that point, he wouldn't be able to believe any open proclamations about his merits and talents. So I stayed with his pain for a number of sessions. And then, when he seemed a little less depressed by his loss, I said: "You know what kills me, Tom? It's that the rotten politics have deprived those students of the tremendous, creative programs that you would have introduced for them. And the terrific role model that they would have had in you. It's a damn shame!"

Tom gave a little smile—partly at my outburst, but mostly, I feel, because I had heard his deepest pain and had validated his self-worth.

4. Giving an Adequate Response

The final condition for good listening is that I make an adequate response to what you have shared with me. This final step is essential. When you're hurting, you need a warm, caring response to show you that I understand and care. It is not sufficient that I understand internally. That doesn't touch you, unless I show it to you in a clear and adequate way. You need to know that I understand your feelings. You need to have concrete evidence that I don't blame you for them before you can stop blaming yourself.

When I fail to give you very clear signs that I do understand, you are left in an awful quandary. And, almost immediately, you start thinking the worst: that

I am judging you, that I think that you're an awful person for having those kinds of feelings. My silence makes you feel blamed.

So, it is imperative that I make an adequate response to you. How? How do I do that? Do I have to make a beautiful speech? Or, present you with an instant solution to your problem? Do I have to give you some immediate sedative for your pain? No. Not at all! My response can be just a simple exclamation: "Wow, that's really rough!" or "Gee, I'm awfully sorry!" That genuine, feeling response is much more effective than a long speech. What really counts is not the words but the feelings that I have for you and the tone of voice that shows that I understand.

Or my response might be a warm gesture without any words at all. Taking your hand and squeezing it. Taking you in my arms and holding you. It might be just showing you by the pained look on my face that I feel so very much for you. The big thing is that I understand your pain, that I feel badly for you, that I care!

Some years ago I worked with a young priest, Dan, who had been very depressed since the death of his mother a few years before. What made it harder for him was that his dad remarried, and the young priest just couldn't take to the second wife. As a result, he went home much less often. This hurt his dad a great deal. He loved Dan and hated to see him pulling away. So he made arrangements for the three of them to go on vacation to a place in the Catskills where they used to go when Dan's mother was alive. Dan dreaded going back there, especially with his stepmother. But he appreciated how much his dad was trying to keep their old closeness, so he agreed to go.

When they got to the place, however, a wave of nostalgia overcame Dan. He excused himself and went to the cottage that they used to rent when his mother was alive. He sat down on the steps with his head in his hands. Memories from the past flooded over him like a torrent. After a short while his dad came along and sat down beside him. And for about twenty minutes, they both sat there in silence. Then his dad put his arm around his shoulder and he said: "Dan, I know how you feel. I know. I loved her too!" And they both sat there and cried—unashamedly.

That's listening! That man could have said many hurtful things to his son, if he had stayed in his own world. He easily could have blamed him for spoiling the vacation. Or he could have tried to force him to focus on his stepmother's feelings. But this man knew how to listen. He put aside his own point of view for the moment and took on his son's point of view. And in doing that, he felt his son's pain.

The young priest told me later: "Jim, I never loved him so much, as I did at that moment!" This is not surprising. It means so much to us to be heard and understood. Good listening is such an act of loving that we can even substitute it for the word "love" in St. Paul's magnificent passage from First Corinthians (1 Cor 13). Consider the passage rewritten in this way:

I may be able to speak the languages of human beings and even of angels, but if I don't listen, my speech is no more that a noisy gong or a clanging bell. I may have the gift of inspired preaching; I may have all knowledge and understand all secrets; I may have all the faith needed to move mountains—but if I do not listen, I am nothing. I may give away everything I have, and even give my body to be burned—but if I do not listen, it does me no good.

Listening is patient and kind; it is not jealous or conceited or proud; listening is not ill-mannered or selfish or irritable; listening does not keep a record of wrongs; listening is not happy with evil, but is happy with the truth. Listening never gives up; and its faith, hope and patience never fail. . . .

It is when we learn to listen with sensitivity and concern that we truly learn to love!

Consider again the four crucial steps to good listening:

1. Stepping out of my own world
2. Stepping into your world
3. Sensing your deepest feelings
4. Giving an adequate response

Can you think of one or two people you have known who were especially skilled listeners? Describe the ways in which they put these steps into practice.

CHAPTER 9

Understanding Our Listening Tools

I realize at this point that when I do anything to increase your self-esteem, I give you a gift much more precious than gold. I give you the wondrous gift of yourself: beautiful, warm appreciation of your beauty and your goodness which is really the heart of all true happiness. And, conversely, when I do anything to lessen your self-esteem, even in a limited way, I strike you where you are most vulnerable. I cause you very painful and humiliating feelings.

It has also become clear that the mechanism that can most quickly erode and destroy your self-esteem is the deadly mechanism of blame. When I communicate blame, I smash into your self-esteem like a hail of deadly arrows, causing you all kinds of pain and making you feel guilty and ugly. And, I thus set off within you a strong, insistent urge to punish yourself, a vague feeling that you have to pay back for all your "evil."

And, as incongruous as it seems, most times you have done nothing to justify my blame. You have not been vicious or hateful. You have done nothing to hurt me. The problem is all my "stuff": my ugly mood, my unrealistic demands, my lack of sensitivity. Nevertheless, my blame is the spark that sets off that fearful dynamite which is always there within you, just waiting to explode.

Probably the form that blame takes most often is poor listening: my insensitivity when you need to be heard, my preoccupation with other matters when you're hurting and just hunger for someone to understand and care. I don't have to blame you directly to strike at your self-esteem. All I have to do is not listen to you. That gives you the very same ugly message: "You're not worth my time! You can't possibly have anything worthwhile to say!" And you feel guilt, as though it were you who were insensitive, instead of me.

I can cause you terrible pain, and I can do it so easily and unwittingly! When I see the power I have, I want to take the steps necessary so that I will never cause this kind of pain again. I want to follow the example related in the last chapter, the example of Dan's father. He did all the right things and he did them beautifully. The result was a wonderful healing that meant the world to both of them.

VIVID CONTRAST

It helps my appreciation of good listening when I contrast that example with what happens so often when you and I hurt each other. When that happens, we both feel such pain that we don't want to deal with anything except our own pain. Neither one of us will leave our own world. We each feel that we have to make the other person understand and apologize.

I'm not saying that those feelings aren't understandable. They certainly are. The guilt that we feel from the "blame" of being misunderstood is so very painful that we have the strongest impulse to get rid of it as soon as we can.

That's what's so sad! Both of us have a valid need to be heard. The sad part is that we both need to be heard at the same time. So, neither one of us wants to listen. Both feel frustrated and alienated from the other. It happens so often—a painful, no-win situation.

I have to become very aware of these emotional "stand-offs" in my own life. One of us has to break the deadlock and listen first. I must train myself to take that role.

I can readily see that this is the hardest part of good listening—this difficult passage from my world to yours. It takes a strong and deliberate effort on my part to postpone the satisfaction for which I hunger, my longing that you first understand me. I have to make it a goal for myself that I will be there first to understand you.

TOOLS OF COMMUNICATION

There is another reason, however, why it is so difficult for me to enter your world. It isn't only my reluctance to leave my own world. I also lack a sufficient familiarity with our communication tools. Even when

I am very sincerely determined to see things from your point of view, I am still very prone to misunderstand you because I am not familiar with the manner in which you express your thoughts and feelings.

It's important, therefore, that I study the process of human communication, that I become familiar with the tools that you and I have been given to express ourselves to each other. They are the only tools we have, and, unfortunately, they are very limited tools.

WHY SPECIAL TOOLS?

You may wonder: "Why do we need special tools for communication?" For the simple reason that we are completely cut off and alienated from one another's thoughts and feelings. We may be present to each other physically, but in our thoughts and feelings, we are as much alone, as if we were in separate, dark dungeon cells—as if we were each in solitary confinement.

We cannot see each other's thoughts. We cannot perceive each other's feelings. The only way that we can get through to each other is by a complicated system of signals—coded signals—somewhat like the dots and dashes of the Morse code. Whether we realize it or not, every message that we send to each other is in code: a code that I myself have set up, a code that almost always is different from your code. In a very real sense, we are like the people at the tower of Babel. We are all speaking a different language!

In heaven this will all be different, because in heaven we will see each other's minds and hearts. I'll see your thoughts as clearly and directly as I can now see your face. And you'll see my feelings as clearly as you see me right now before you. It will be beautiful, because then there will be no more misunderstandings.

Until we get to heaven, however, we have to settle for our primitive tools and our often contradictory signals. That's the second reason why listening and understanding are so hard for us. Okay then, let's take a look at our tools and see what we can do to make the best of them. What are our tools for communication? We have three essential tools. We might call them our transmitter, our decoder, and our clarifier.

My Transmitter

First of all, I have a transmitter to send out my message. What are the signals that I use? The most important of all are my words. But facial expressions, tears, laughter, and tone of voice all come into play. My gestures are also part of my signal system—the way I stand, the way I look, whether or not I look at you, even the way I breathe, and, above all, the over-all attitude that I communicate.

All of these are signals from me to you that enable you to get a picture of my inner world. These signals express outwardly and in code what I think and feel inwardly.

MY DECODER

The second tool I have is my decoder, the tool I use in order to interpret and understand the meaning of the signals that you are sending out to me. I have to decode your signals if I am going to understand your message.

My ears can hear what you are saying and the tone of voice in which you say it. My eyes can see the look on your face, the attitude that you seem to have. I can perceive your signals with my eyes and my ears. But, what do all these signals mean? What is the message that you are sending me through these signals? My eyes and ears cannot tell me that. The work of deciphering your signals is the work of my decoder, the work of my mind and my heart!

What am I saying? I'm saying that *everything* that you transmit to me is in code. Your signals must be decoded before they can have any meaning at all. For example, suppose I frown. What does that mean? It could mean many different things. It could signify that I disapprove of what you are doing. It could also mean that I am confused. My frown could also signify pain on my part. The same signal can signify many different thoughts and feelings. What it actually does signify depends upon the meaning that I give to it. It depends upon my code!

Or, I put both of my hands to my head. What does this mean? It could mean that I am angry. It could also signify that I am elated. It could also reveal frustration.

Or, again, I stand before you with my arms folded. What does this signal mean? It could mean that I feel shy or afraid. It could also signify a warning: "Listen here, mister! You'd better shape up, or else!" It could even show aloofness. My silence could be a sign that I am sincerely listening to you. But it could also be a sign that I am angry or a sign that I am bored.

Our words, our facial expressions, our gestures—indeed all our signals, can signify many widely different meanings. Even our smiles can have different meanings, sometimes exact *opposite* meanings! My smile can mean that I am happy or that I am sad and trying to cover it up. It can express affection and it can express hate: "I've got you now!"

This is why the job of decoding is one of the most important parts of listening. It is so evident to me now why I have to enter your world: because your signals have no clear meaning for me until I know your code!

My biggest temptation, as we saw, is for me to interpret your signals with my code rather than with yours, to stay in my own world and interpret things from my point of view. When I do that, I don't hear you at all! Your signals have no meaning. If I force my meaning onto them, I miss your message. And I misinterpret your feelings.

And, so, for example, if people in my past life have used tears in order to make me feel guilty and to manipulate me, what happens when I now see your tears? Almost surely I will interpret them in exactly the same way. I think that you are trying to play on my sympathy. And I miss your distress completely! Instead of understanding your pain and feeling empathy for you, I see your tears as nothing more than a clever trick to control me. And instead of feeling your pain with you, I get furious at your "manipulation."

BREAKDOWN OF COMMUNICATION

This is where our communication most often breaks down. I say to you, "You look a little tired. Have you been sick?" And, according to my code, that means: "I care about you. I want to help." But my comment sounds to you like I'm saying that you look haggard or old. So, instead of feeling good, you feel resentful of my insult. You heard my message from your point of view when it has to be heard from my point of view. Why? Because it is my message. I'm the one who gives my signals their meaning.

Or, take the example where a husband comes home late from work. What does that signal mean? It could mean many things. It could mean that he was out drinking with his friends. It could mean that he is sick of being with his wife, so he stays out as long as he can. It could even mean that he's seeing another woman on the side. It could mean all those things that would get his wife furious.

But, it could also signify situations that are perfectly innocent, including the fact that he had to work late, that he was out searching for a nice present for his wife's birthday, or that one of his fellow workers got sick and he volunteered to take him home. So his wife has to be very careful not to presuppose that she has the right code. She must wait until she is sure that she knows what his real message is.

At the beginning of one of our group meetings at the office, Paul, a man in his early forties, pulled his chair back from the circle and sat almost sideways to the other members of the group. A number of the members reacted to Paul's signal with anger. Who did he think he was! They just presupposed that it was arrogance on his part or a feeling of superiority. But it wasn't that at all. He was scared stiff of the other members and, indeed, of the whole group process. They used their code instead of trying to discover his. So they failed to enter his world.

MY CLARIFIER

How can I be sure that I'm getting your real message? Do I have any tool to help me to discover what your code is? I have to find out what your code is, because only then can I interpret your signals correctly and enter your world. I can do this with the help of my third tool, my clarifier.

In some ways, my clarifier is my most important tool. It is my ability to check out both my own decoder and yours. That is, it enables me to understand just how you are interpreting my signals and how I am interpreting yours. So, it offers me my best chance to enter into your world. And it is my best tool for getting you to understand me.

In other words, it gives me the chance to make sure that you are interpreting my signals correctly, that you are interpreting my signals with *my* code. So, for example, when I told you that you looked tired and I saw that you looked hurt, I can check out with you exactly what you heard. I can say: "Gee, you look hurt by what I said. That was awfully insensitive of me." And then after I've let you feel my real regrets, I can say: "I just want you to know that I'm here and that I care."

What have I done? I've clarified for myself what your signal meant, i.e., why you looked hurt. I realized how you interpreted my words in a very negative way. And second, I've clarified for you exactly what my real message was.

A SAMPLE CODED MESSAGE

Let me send you a message using a simple code and see how well you interpret it. Here it is:

Smzatyxynotugbherceosmpebazgoruenartjlkirsht-dewncekr!

I'll bet you are finding it very difficult to make any sense out of it. That's understandable. It looks like gibberish. How can you possibly understand its meaning until you know the code in which it was written? How can you do that? Since it is my message, you simply have to ask me! And when I tell you that the code is every second letter, it is very easy for you to get the correct message: "May you become a great listener!"

So, we can never really be sure what the other person's message is until we have checked it out and clarified what meaning the person intended to give to his or her signals. Let's never fail to clarify: "Am I hearing you correctly? Is this what you're saying?"

Or if I'm the one who is talking and I'm not sure that you're hearing me correctly, I can ask: "How did you hear what I just said? You look angry. Did you feel that I was putting you down?"

Or, "Honestly, I don't feel your plan will work, but that doesn't mean that I don't like you or that I don't appreciate all the trouble you went to in writing it up. I appreciate that very much! I'm very grateful that you're so interested." Clarify! Clarify! Clarify! It can save us so much misunderstanding and pain.

CONCLUSION

I can only really hear you, therefore, when I enter your world and see things from your point of view. No easy task! At the outset, I'm not only convinced that my own point of view is the only true one, but I also lack an understanding of how you express yourself, especially the fact that you express yourself in code. As a result, I read your signals for the meaning that those signals have for me! That's simply another way of my staying in my own world instead of entering into yours.

The key step for me to take in order to enter your world is to discover your code. That's where your message lies. It is only there that I can find you and understand you. When I fail to appreciate that, I miss you completely.

It is so important for me to see that our signals—both yours and mine—can mean many, many different things. I just cannot know what your signals mean simply by observing them on the surface. I can guess, but I can't be sure. In one way or other, I have to clarify again and again.

Now that I have some insight about the tools that I have for communication, I have to work on learning how to use them with greater skill!

QUESTIONS FOR REFLECTION

1. Can you think of a specific instance in which you have been misinterpreted by someone who failed to correctly interpret your "code"?

2. Consider again the following clarifying questions:
   • "Am I hearing you correctly? Is that what you're saying?"
   • "How did you hear what I just said? You look angry. Did you feel I was putting you down?"
   • "I'm not sure I understand what you mean."

   Would you feel comfortable using these exact wordings? If not, can you think of others that would work better for you?

CHAPTER 10

Refining Our Skills

We are born with the tools for communication, but we are not born with communication skills. Skills have to be learned with hard work and practice. We don't make a man into a carpenter when we hand him a hammer and a saw. Nor do I turn a person into an artist simply by giving her an easel and some paint. Rubenstein had the inspiration to be a great pianist, but he only became great through effort, through constant study and exhausting practice.

A DIFFICULT TASK

The same is true of communication skills. Acquiring those skills is probably more difficult than acquiring any other, mainly because our tools for communication are limited and are prone to misinterpretation and mistakes. This is really tragic because the art of reaching other human beings in clear understanding and compassion is certainly more important for us to master than any other art. I need you to understand me and feel with me. You need me to understand you.

So, as difficult as it is, we must try to use and refine our communication tools in the most accurate manner that we can. What can we do? We can begin by studying where and how our individual tools are most prone to error, and then be on guard against those possible mistakes. Some of these areas we have seen already, but let's look at each one of our tools in detail.

OUR TRANSMITTER

Sometimes my biggest problem in communicating clearly is a problem with the kind of signals my transmitter sends out to you. Too often my signals are not clear and precise. I want to let you know that your remarks have hurt me, but instead of telling you that I feel hurt, I attack you. I say: "You have some nerve talking to me like that!" Bad signal! I don't know for sure what you really meant or what your motives were. You may not have intended to hurt me at all. All I know for sure is that I feel hurt. So that's exactly what I should say. "Hey, that really hurt!" Then you know how I feel without your feeling put-down or defensive. And you can respond to my pain with care and empathy. Or, if you did mean to hurt me, you can explain exactly why you are upset with me and we can talk it out.

Or, I want to tell you that I think you were courageous in standing up for what you thought was right. So I say to you: "Boy, you really hung in there like a bulldog!" Very poor signal! You may not hear that as courage. You may think that I am saying that you are thick and stubborn. I've used a poor signal, an insensitive choice of word. I should have said: "I think that you have great courage. You are open to what others have to say, but you don't let them force you into accepting their ideas until you are really convinced!" A much better signal. Now you are much more likely to get my message clearly.

Double Signals

Sometimes my signals are confusing to you because I give you mixed signals—signals that give a double and conflicting message. So, for example, I want you to know that I feel very lonely and depressed. I say the words: "lonely" and "depressed," but I give off a nervous laugh when I say them. Or I smile as though I don't really mean what I am saying. As a result, you are confused. One signal is expressing "pain," but the other is expressing "joy." So you are not sure what I really mean or how I really feel.

Why does this happen so often? Especially since I have an almost insatiable desire that you appreciate what I am feeling. I don't want you to be confused about me. I want you to know me.

Then why do I send out such garbled signals? The answer, of course, is my fear—my fear of rejection. I do want you to know me, but I am terrified that you will misunderstand me—that you'll think that I'm a crybaby who is making a big fuss over nothing.

So, when I start to tell you how I feel, my fear makes me smile and laugh nervously so that you'll think that I am only joking about my pain. Now you can't say that I'm a crybaby. I'm making it appear that I'm only kidding around. It's sad! I show a real lack of reverence for my pain, as though it were something trivial. And I also confuse you so badly that you have no idea what I am really feeling.

A Typical Example

Years ago, there were five of us having lunch in the rectory. After lunch, one of the priests said in a very matter-of-fact kind of way: "Would anyone care to go for a walk?" I didn't particularly feel like it and neither did the others. About ten minutes later, he came to my room, unbelievably upset! "You're some Christian!" he shouted at me. "A guy is in pain and you don't give a damn!"

I was dumbfounded! And I felt guilty. I immediately thought that I must have missed the clues that he was in such pain. I told him how sorry I was and, fortunately, he sat down and we talked it all out. There was no doubt that he was hurting terribly, but his signals were woefully inadequate. The pressure of his pain made him feel that he was really crying out for help, but his fear so completely blunted his call for help that his cry wasn't even a whimper.

This happens so often! In one of our group sessions at the Consultation Center, the executive of a large corporation told the group about flying back from a convention where he was terribly criticized by his junior executives. He said in a very noncommittal tone: "Yeah, I didn't care if the plane landed or crashed!"

Nobody heard him! The group went right on talking as though nothing painful had been said. I waited a few minutes and then I asked: "Did anyone hear what Joe said? He said that it made no difference to him whether his plane landed or crashed!" They all fell silent, ashamed that they had missed it. At that moment, Joe could hold it in no longer. He began to shake with sobs. Now his pain was very clear.

The difference in the reaction of the group was remarkable! They were so attentive and understanding. They felt very bad for Joe, and they showed it. Those junior executives had some nerve not to appreciate someone with Joe's sincerity and ability. It was a beautiful outpouring of understanding and care. Joe was visibly and deeply touched by them. It made all the difference in the world when Joe used clear and adequate signals to express how he felt!

We have to be sure that we send out clear, appropriate, coordinated signals—precise words that express exactly what I'm feeling at the moment, appropriate facial expressions, and, especially, appropriate tone of voice.

My outward signals must be an exact reflection of my inner feelings and all of them must be saying the same thing, portraying the same message. Then you have a fighting chance to understand me and to feel with me.

OUR DECODER

While poor signals cause a lot of our problems in communication, the majority of our problems come from a poor use of our second tool, from poor decoding of other people's signals. This is my biggest stumbling block in hearing the real you. I'm overwhelmingly tempted to interpret your signals with my code rather than with yours, to read them according to my point of view, to see them from the vantage point of my world instead of your world. When I do that, I miss you; I only hear me!

The very best and kindest of us fall into this temptation. It's so natural for us to see everything from our own point of view. It takes a strong, deliberate, conscious choice to make me put aside my point of view and see what you are saying through your eyes. It takes a constant, heightened awareness. And it takes continuous practice.

You are laughing nervously. I realize that, when I do that, I'm very anxious. Maybe, maybe, that's what it means in your case. But I can't be sure. So I mustn't conclude that your code is the same as mine. I can ask you: "Are you okay?" and see if you offer me any clarification about what you are feeling.

Or you are crying. What does that mean? I mustn't jump to the conclusion that you are very sad, simply because I cry when I am sad. Your tears could be tears of joy about some wonderful news that you just heard. Or you might be very touched by something beautiful that you just read. I don't really understand until I discover your code. If I am really going to be there for you—hear you and understand you—I simply must get into your world. I must consciously, deliberately choose to see your experiences from your point of view.

Personal Conflict

As we have seen, this is always difficult. However, it is almost a superhuman task when you and I have suffered a mutual misunderstanding: when you accuse me of selfishness or bad intentions that I never had. That blame from you hurts me so much that all I want to do is to make you listen to me and understand me. I want to tell you: "I'm not selfish. I was planning the whole meeting just so people would recognize you and all that you have done." I desperately need you to see that and to acknowledge it!

Right now, it's very hard for me to think about the pain you say that I caused you. I can't feel your pain. I can only feel my own. My own pain is screaming too loudly for me to hear you. All I want to do is to correct your misperceptions of me. I want to be validated. I want relief.

The problem is that you are in exactly the same boat. You're hurting too. And you need the same kind of understanding from me that I need from you. Neither one of us is to be blamed. We are both victims, both in great need of understanding.

I must make myself realize this! Someone has to break the ice. I realize that it must be me. I'm in a better position to know what has happened between us. I want to blame you, but you are not to blame. You are in every bit as much pain as I am. Hurt. Bewildered. Feeling betrayed by me. I must make myself hear that and feel that.

When I do make myself listen to you, the rewards are unspeakable! You begin to feel so relieved that you can relax and begin to understand me also. We have found each other again.

Our Clarifier

And finally we come to that wonderful and most helpful tool that, unfortunately, I tend to use least of all—my clarifier, my ability to check out how you are hearing me and how I am hearing you. Am I decoding your signals correctly? Or am I reacting to my own distortions, to hurts that you in no way intended to inflict on me?

"Am I hearing you rightly? Is this what you are saying?" "How did you hear what I just said? You look hurt. I hope you did not hear that as a put-down. I'd feel awful, if that's what you thought!"

"Listen, I disagree with part of your plan, but that doesn't mean that I disagree with all of it! I think that it has great merit. And I appreciate so much the time and energy that you put into it!" We simply must take the time to clarify! It allows me to hear you, and it gives you a fighting chance to hear me.

CONCLUSION

Our tools for communication are limited tools. They can be fraught with misreadings and misunderstandings. But they are the only tools that we have. Our best approach is not to waste our time regretting their limitations but to use them in the most careful way that we can, to watch for those areas where they are most likely to lead us astray.

If I really appreciate what an unspeakably healing power good listening is, then no limitation can keep me back from making the best effort I can.

QUESTIONS FOR REFLECTION

1. Have you found yourself sending mixed signals, perhaps joking or laughing about your feelings as if they are unimportant?

2. Can you describe a specific situation in which you misunderstood someone because you failed to clarify what he or she was saying?

CHAPTER 11

The Main Types of Communication

There are several different types of communication, each one of which is intended to accomplish a definite goal. When we greet each other in the morning, for example, it is only as a "passing-the-time-of-day" kind of thing. "Good morning. How are you? Enjoy your day." We don't expect anything more of this type of communication than a polite acknowledgment of each other's presence.

There is also a similar type of communication which might be called "small talk" or "chitchat." This is the kind of talk we use when waiting in line in the supermarket or when riding with an acquaintance on a bus. We comment on current events or on last night's television show. We don't bring up anything personal or deeply meaningful.

Occasionally, a person will bring up deep problems and hurts in a small-talk situation, forgetting that this is not the setting for this type of problem. This is really a mistake and it is bound to lead to further frustration.

In a small-talk setting, there is neither the time nor the privacy to deal with real pain, so the outcome is usually very poor. The person we confide in feels awkward and embarrassed and quite uncertain about how to reply. We must understand and respect the purpose for each type of communication, even small talk.

THREE MAIN TYPES

There are three other types of communication that are very important to us and which are intended to accomplish very definite goals.

There is (1) advice, (2) persuasion, and (3) (the type of communication that we have been studying closely up to now) the self-revelation. Let's look at each.

ADVICE

Advice is a valid type of communication, although it has certain definite limitations and restrictions. Advice is the guidance that I request from you about an area of knowledge where you have greater learning and experience. I ask you to give me the benefit of your knowledge on how I should proceed with a particular problem. If you're a licensed electrician, for example, I may very well ask you where I should put the hot wire and where to put the neutral one.

My request makes sense. You have greater knowledge in this field than I do, so you can keep me from making foolish mistakes. And in no way do I resent your telling me what to do. On the contrary, I welcome it, because your advice can help me with my problem.

Advice, however, can be fraught with problems. Because advisors have a certain expertise in their field of competence, they can be tempted to think that they are experts in other fields as well. And they can start giving advice in areas where they do not have expertise. Because I am an accomplished electrician does not mean that I am an expert marriage counselor. So, when I leave the field of electricity and start telling you how to live your marriage, I am way out of line. And you have every right to resent it.

Again, advisors get so used to giving advice that they can be tempted to offer it, even when it is not requested. When I do that to you, you can't help but resent it. Your space has been invaded. You feel violated.

And finally, I must realize that advice is advice, nothing more. It is not a set of orders that you must follow. Even though you asked for my advice, the final decision on how you act is always in your hands. And I should never resent the fact that you didn't follow my recommendations. I have no right to take away your privilege of self-determination.

I must be careful to check myself on these points because it is very easy for me to try to force my opinions on you or to get angry at you if you do not follow my advice. Your decision is your right and privilege. I am not in charge of your life!

The second big type of communication is persuasion. Persuasion is an effort on my part to get you to agree with my ideas or with my plan of action. Persuasion is communication which is mainly task-oriented. It deals with ideas and plans of action, and the goal is to reach as much agreement as possible. The success of persuasion lies in the greatness of the agreement that you and I can reach.

So, in persuasion I tell you my ideas as clearly as possible, offering you the best reasons I can think of to convince you to agree with me or to follow my plan of action. I try to motivate you by offering you reasons that I know are attractive to you.

So, for example, I may try to persuade my wife that we should save in order to buy ourselves a new home. I know that she loves going on vacations and eating out twice a week, so asking her to give up those joys in order to save is one of the difficulties that I will have to overcome. In order to persuade her, I may describe the joy of having our own place, the satisfaction of our being able to decorate it just the way we like and to entertain our friends in style.

Or, as a school principal, I may propose a plan to the staff that we should start school at 7:30 a.m. and dismiss for the day at 12:30. Then, I point out, no one would have to take lunch duty and we'd have the entire afternoon free: two points that I know the staff will find very attractive.

THE IMPORTANCE OF PERSUASION

Persuasion is a very important type of communication. We use persuasion in trying to spread the faith, in trying to get welfare reforms and better mental health programs. We us persuasion to try to get our friends to go to AA, to inspire ideals of reverence and respect in children, to bring people back to the church. This book, in fact, is a form of persuasion, trying to convince the reader of the beauty of our power to listen and the good that it can do. The Acts of the Apostles says that: "Paul tried by every kind of argument and persuasion to convince the people to accept the Lord Jesus."

THE LIMITATIONS OF PERSUASION

Like advice, however, persuasion can also be abused. While it is perfectly fair for me to try to get you to agree with my point of view, it is vitally important that in no way do I ever impinge upon your freedom. The use of force—either physical or moral force—changes persuasion into manipulation, which is a frightful act of irreverence!

Also, when I am trying to persuade, I try to get you to do something which is for your good, or for the good of both of us. But, I must carefully avoid even the slightest suggestion that you are bad or stupid if you don't agree with my point of view. I may even offer you reasons for the opposite view, leaving you free to make your own decision. I show you how badly I feel that your smoking has left you with a chronic cough.

Manipulation is very different! In manipulation, I don't consider you at all. I try to get you to do something that is for my convenience, even though it is not good for you. I convince you to drive me shopping when I know that you are dead tired and need to rest. There's no care for you. The only thing that counts is my convenience. Manipulation is selfish to the core.

A common form of manipulation is the use of "scare tactics," in the form of either fear or guilt. I threaten to expose some secret that you have been hiding if you don't do what I want you to do. That's a terrible abuse! Or, I may try to make you feel guilty by telling you that you are selfish and insensitive for not doing what I'm asking you to do.

It's unbelievable how often this happens. People twist their friends' feelings by emotional pain to make them conform to their will. Such cruelty is a far cry from persuasion. Persuasion leaves persons free, free to make up their own minds and to follow their own decisions.

When engaging in persuasion, I maintain a real reverence both for you and for myself. I try to get you to see that a certain course of action is the best course of action for us both. And I am open to listen to your ideas on the subject.

TASK-ORIENTED

Since persuasion is task-oriented, the measure of my success in this kind of communication is how much I get you to agree with me, or, how much you convince me to agree with you. What really counts is the amount of agreement that we achieve.

It's important that I realize that the purpose of persuasion is not to prove that my ideas or plans are better than yours. It is not to demonstrate that I am a superior person to you. The goal of persuasion is agreement and truth!

I'm not less worthwhile as a person if I should discover that, in this case, your ideas are better than my own. I'm only less a person if I'm not big enough to admit that. Persuasion is not a "win-or-lose" proposition. It is a search for the greatest amount of agreement that we can achieve.

An Aid to Persuasion

Quite often, complete agreement seems impossible to achieve. You have a firm commitment to your plan; I have a commitment to mine. What can we do? How can we resolve our differences and get the task done?

To accomplish this, we both need a special tool called "compromise," the flexibility to be able to give up a little in order to get a little.

For example, I'd like a friend to join me for a week's vacation in Florida. But he is very conscientious about his job and feels that a week is longer than he wants to be away. I remind him that we have very competent people to take his place, and that he's got to let himself get away for a while and relax, that it will do us both a world of good.

He wants to go along with me. He knows that we both would enjoy it, but he can't allow himself to be away that long. We just sincerely and honestly disagree. Is it hopeless? No, not with compromise! I say to him: "Okay, then, how about going for a long weekend?" I really want the whole week, but I'm willing to give up the extra days in order to enjoy the time that we can have. I'm respecting what I would like, and I am also respecting his feelings about his job.

I used to think of compromise as a cowardly thing, but that was because I thought of it in terms of sacrificing one's principles. That would be cowardly! But, as it is used here, it simply means giving up one convenience in order to gain another one.

SELF-REVELATION

Finally, the most important type of communication is the communication of self-revelation. This type of communication is about feelings, and our goal here is not necessarily agreement, but rather, acceptance, understanding, and care.

In this most noble type of communication, I am not out to convince you to agree with my ideas or to follow my plan of action. It's nice for me if you do agree that my feelings are appropriate. But you don't have to agree in order to understand and affirm my feelings. Self-revelation, in other words, is not task-oriented. It is person-oriented! The only goal of self-revelation is to be understood and affirmed.

All you have to do is to understand that this is the way I feel—that I feel lonely and sad or frustrated or put down. Or that I feel very happy. You understand and you do not try to talk me out of my feelings, even if you think that I am overreacting and that, therefore, my feelings are inappropriate.

This is not a case of your leaving me with false perceptions. Eventually, when I am ready to hear you, you may suggest that I overreacted in this situation—that I was perhaps carrying with me a lot of anger from the past. But you know that I can't hear that right now. I'm in too much pain. So, right now, you meet me where I can hear you. You let me know that you understand how much I am hurting and you share it all with me.

For example, suppose that you are a high school teacher and that you lose your temper and strike one of your students. You tell me later how terribly guilty and depressed you feel about it. It opened a hornet's nest. The principal is on your back. The parents are going to take you to court. You feel foolish and stupid that you let a fresh kid make you lose your cool.

I understand all those awful feelings and feel so bad for you. I can't agree that what you did was the right thing. It wasn't! But, I can understand how exasperating a student can become to a teacher. I can feel with you, your anger and frustration, and let you know that I understand how easily this could happen. And I can reassure you that you are an excellent teacher—that this incident in no way takes away from that excellence.

This is what you really need. You don't need me to lie and say that what you did was perfectly all right. You, yourself, know that it wasn't! You need me to understand and care.

THE BIG MISTAKE

One of the big mistakes that we make in self-revelation is to confuse self-revelation with persuasion. To think, for example, that to have you understand me means that I have to get you to agree with me! This is simply not so. I can understand my teacher friend and feel very deeply for him, even though I certainly could not agree that he did the right thing.

Years ago, a priest in one of our groups at the office made this mistake. He was a very conscientious parish priest who, along with his other duties, went into the school each week to teach religion. The principal of the school, however, was a stickler for regulations. She ran an excellent school, but was hard on the teachers and also on the parish priests. If the priests did not arrive at class exactly on time, she wouldn't allow them to teach.

One day, this particular priest, Richard, came to the group fuming! He was delayed at the rectory for a few minutes, and the principal refused to let him teach. He was wild, and expressed to the group his frustration and his anger. "She should be thrown out of the school!" he yelled. "She's a rigid legalist who is a horrible example to the children!"

To his great surprise, no one in the group responded. He seemed so frustrated. So he repeated his call for the principal's dismissal. No reaction. He was devastated.

I allowed the feelings to stay in that tension for a few minutes and then I intervened. I said to the group: "How do you feel about what happened to Richard?" The response was tremendous! They were furious at the principal and very hurt for Richard and the humiliation she had put him through. Richard was deeply touched. At last, he felt understood and affirmed in his feelings.

His big mistake was in thinking that he had to make them agree that the principal was an unfit educator. They couldn't do that because it just wasn't true. She was rigid and unbending, but her overall score as an educator was very high.

Richard confused self-revelation with persuasion, and it caused him a great deal of pain and frustration. The group could feel very deeply for him without agreeing with his idea that the principal should be barred from the school.

CONCLUSION

In summary, then, persuasion is my attempt to convince you to agree with my ideas. The main area of our discussion is the area of ideas, and the goal is agreement. The greater the area of agreement, the more successful has been our communication.

Self-revelation, on the other hand, centers on the area of feelings. Here, my goal is not to change your ideas, not to persuade you to take any definite course of action. Here, my goal is to have you understand me and affirm me.

It is so important, therefore, that I understand this point—that I understand exactly what I need from our conversation, and that I make clear to you my precise needs. I can say to you, for example: "Pete, I need you to listen to me. I have an awful lot of mixed-up feelings. I'm not sure that I'm reacting right to that guy, but his remarks really upset me. I just need you to understand!" I'm helping you to know my code, helping you to be there for me where I need you most.

And I must do the same for you. What is it that you need at this moment? Are you trying to convince me to help you with some favorite project? Or do you just need me to be there with you in your feelings and understand what you are going through? When this is your real need, I can put aside all questions about agreement and go right to the heart of your pain.

1. Have you ever found yourself expressing a powerful feeling in the context of casual small talk? What were the results?

2. Have you ever found yourself becoming angry because someone decided against taking your advice?

CHAPTER 12

The Healing Power

It has caused me great sadness to see the pain people have to suffer without any good reason, the huge amount of guilt and shame that is heaped upon us without any wrongdoing on our part. The unrealistic expectations of others make us feel ugly; their surliness makes us feel that there must be something wrong with us. It's such a gross injustice! We probably suffer more from this neurotic guilt than from any real guilt on our part.

In no way am I denying the possibility or the presence of real guilt in our lives! To be mature adults, we must assume responsibility for our words and actions. And when we deliberately do things that hurt others and put them down, then we certainly should feel guilty. We should apologize and make amends.

However, for most of us, there is probably very little deliberate cruelty that we do to others. But, that doesn't mean that we do not suffer these terrible pangs of shame and lowered self-esteem. So often, we too are literally tortured by neurotic guilt.

It's a thrilling feeling for me then to realize that I have power! Power to reverse these neurotic trends in myself. And the glorious power to heal some of these painful wounds in you! I can be there for you when you are really hurting. I can let you know that I understand, that I care! My careful listening can ease the painful pressure of your bursting feelings and let you feel again some measure of peace. Most of all, I can give you the overwhelming comfort that your feelings are okay, that you are okay! *It's not something that I am making up.* It's the truth! I'm just helping you to see it and feel it!

It's an overwhelming thought that I have the power to do this. What a privilege! And, what a responsibility! I feel guilty that I have not used this awesome power to its full capacity. I just know that, more than anything else, I want to be a good listener from now on. I want to be a healer.

It makes sense to me, then, that I should start by first trying to discover the reasons why I have failed in the past. What have I done wrong? What steps have I failed to take? For most of us, the biggest problem has been our overriding preoccupation with ourselves. As much as I hate to admit it, that's the big problem. I've been preoccupied with my thoughts, my point of view, my hurts and hunger for understanding! I allowed all my "stuff" to fill my mind and heart until there was no room for you or your pain.

It's not that my needs are not sacred also. But, if I am going to be the kind of listener who really heals, then I simply have to get out of my own world when I am listening to you. I simply cannot hear you from my world. I must enter yours!

I must try to discover your point of view, what your signals really mean, the code that you are using to express your feelings. Only then can I know what you are feeling and feel it with you—and let you know that it's okay.

No Easy Task

I know that this is no easy task. And facing that reality will be a help to me. But, each of us can resolve to practice every day. When I am in your presence, let me concentrate on giving you my entire attention—study you with my eyes, listen to every word, pay close attention to your tone of voice, observe your attitude, your mood, your whole bearing. Just that close attention will make you feel special. And it will give me an insight into your code and your feelings.

Let me also honestly inquire of my friends about my listening habits. I could say to my close friends: "You know, sometimes I feel that I don't really hear what you are feeling. I regret that. It's so unfair to you!

Is that how I strike you? Have you felt hurt or neglected by anything that I did or didn't do?"

The fact that I am acknowledging that I have some limitations in this way makes it easier for my friends to point out the limitations that they observe. Good friends will do that for me. They will be honest with me and let me know if there are any flaws in my listening pattern. And they will do this for two reasons: because they want to help me and because they want me to listen more accurately to them!

POOR LISTENING

It is also no small help to my motivation for me to realize the absolutely devastating effects that my poor listening has on you. When I fail to listen well, I send you disparaging signals about your self-worth. Even when I have absolutely no intention of hurting you, I can hurt you deeply. I don't like to think that I have caused that kind of pain in you, but I know that I have. Let this painful realization be a real deterrent for me in the future! I want to heal, not to hurt!

MY OWN RELIEF

Being aware of these dynamic forces of our human personality can also be a great help to me in my own struggles with guilt and shame. When people around me are irritable and insensitive, I can make myself realize that the uncomfortable feeling that I have is guilt. I can say to myself: "You feel blamed and unworthy, but you have no right to feel that way! This isn't your problem! You haven't done anything wrong."

Naming my ugly feelings and realizing that they are inappropriate: what a relief! I can then let them go!

COMMITMENT

May each person reading this book find the strength and the courage to pray honestly the following prayer: "Lord, help me to commit myself to this most noble pursuit. And let me never turn back from it. Like you, may I 'go about doing good!' And may people say of me as they, said of you: 'And everyone He touched was healed!'"

QUESTIONS FOR REFLECTION

1. Can you name two specific strategies you can implement to help you move toward being a better listener?

2. Consider including your efforts toward good listening in your journaling or daily spiritual reflection, or begin a practice of daily reflection for that purpose.